THE DIOCESE OF NORTH AMERICA & EUROPE
The Mar Thoma Church

Rt. Rev. Dr. Isaac Mar Philoxenos
Diocesan Bishop

Sinai Mar Thoma Center
2320 S. Merrick Avenue
Merrick, NY 11566
Tel: (516) 377-3311
Fax: (516) 377-3322
Email: marthomadiocese@gmail.com

Dearly beloved in Christ.

Greetings in the name of our Lord Jesus Christ.

I am very happy that the Sunday School revised curriculum of our Diocese is well accepted in all Sunday schools. We appreciate the Diocesan Sunday School Council for the initiative in making it available to teachers as well as students.

At this time, we need to acknowledge the contributions of the pioneers of the Diocesan Sunday School for developing a curriculum, conducive to the culture and practice of the land, without sacrificing the faith, heritage and value system of our church. Revisions were made many a time considering the feedback from teachers and parents. I hope this edition will benefit our children and help them get new insights into the fundamental teachings of the Bible, and the faith and practices of the church.

The motto of our Sunday School is *'Come to Jesus, Bring every child to Jesus'*. It is my prayer that through these lessons, our children may come to a personal encounter with Jesus, make a commitment to follow Him, and bring others to His fold.

May God's blessings be with you all.

Rt. Rev. Dr. Isaac Mar Philoxenos
Diocesan Bishop
June 2020

Acknowledgment

Give ear, O my people, to my teaching; incline your ears to the words of my mouth! 2. I will open my mouth in a parable; I will utter dark sayings from of old, 3. things that we have heard and known, that our fathers have told us. 4. We will not hide them from their children, but tell to the coming generation the glorious deeds of the Lord, and his might, and the wonders that he has done. Psalm 78:1-4

God bless our Sunday school teachers who take the time and effort each week to prepare and teach each lesson with love and patience.

The Diocese owes a debt of gratitude to the Sunday school teachers who made this book possible. I wish to take a moment to thank Dr. T. M. Thomas and team for the first edition, Mrs. Shiby George, Mr. Tom Philip and team for the current edition. Also wish to thank the Mar Thoma Sunday School Samajam, Rev. Ninu Chandy, and Mrs. Madhu Blessy with all the updates and corrections.

On behalf of the Diocesan Sunday schools, I'd like to express our most sincere appreciation to our President, Rt. Rev. Dr. Isaac Mar Philoxenos Episcopa, for his love, prayer and leadership. Also thank Rt. Rev. Dr. Geevarghese Mar Theodosius in providing the vision and leadership for the current curriculum. I would also like to extend my gratitude to the 2017-2020 Diocesan Sunday School Council Members Rev. Larry Varghese, Mr. Thomas Easo, and Mr. George Babu for their long hours of work, commitment, and dedication. We prayerfully welcome the newly (2020-2023) elected council members Mrs. Julie Alex, Mr. George Sam, and Dr. Mathew Sadhu.

The regional representatives have done a great deal of work with the Diocese exam preparations, exam evaluations, VBS, regional conferences, and various mission activities. Please email marthomanae.ss@gmail.com for any suggestions, changes, or updates.

Now to him who is able to do far more abundantly than all that we ask or think, according to the power at work within us, 21. to him be glory in the church and in Christ Jesus throughout all generations, forever and ever. Amen. Ephesians 3:20-21

In His Service!

Reji Alexander

Secretary, Mar Thoma Sunday Schools
[Diocese of North America]
marthomanae.ss@gmail.com

CONTENTS

Lesson 1: Adam and Eve Disobey God

Our disobiedence can separate us from God.

Aim: To understand that God made rules to protect us and that sin entered the world when Adam and Eve broke the rules.

Opening Prayer: Lord, we thank you for saving us from our sins. Help us to be aware of the sin that surrounds us in this world so that we may stand strong against it. Help us to be obedient to your laws and teachings. Continue to show us mercy Lord when we are disobedient, and please forgive us for our sins. Help us to grow stronger in our knowledge of you. In your Holy and precious name we pray. Amen.

Let's Read more about the story from the Bible!
Genesis 3:1-7

Now the serpent was more crafty than any other wild animal that the Lord God had made. He said to the woman, "Did God say, 'You shall not eat from any tree in the garden'?" 2 The woman said to the serpent, "We may eat of the fruit of the trees in the garden; 3 but God said, 'You shall not eat of the fruit of the tree that is in the middle of the garden, nor shall you touch it, or you shall die.'" 4 But the serpent said to the woman, "You will not die; 5 for God knows that when you eat of it your eyes will be opened, and you will be like God,[a] knowing good and evil." 6 So when the woman saw that the tree was good for food, and that it was a delight to the eyes, and that the tree was to be desired to make one wise, she took of its fruit and ate; and she also gave some to her husband, who was with her, and he ate. 7 Then the eyes of both were opened, and they knew that they were naked; and they sewed fig leaves together and made loincloths for themselves.

Things to Remember: Main Ideas from the Lesson

1. Adam and Eve willingly turned away from God by eating the fruit.

   Adam and Eve willingly turned away from God by eating the forbidden fruit. But before either of them ever touched the fruit, they had already sinned in their hearts. Eve had sinned by deciding to eat the fruit. Allowing herself to be influenced by the serpent (who was Satan), Eve began to doubt God and trust herself. Adam had sinned by deciding to let Eve eat the fruit even though God said it would bring death. Then, when Eve did not die right away, Adam ate also. So, in the very first sin, we see people trusting themselves rather than God.

2. God's word proved true, and death entered the garden.
When Adam and Eve sinned, death entered the garden just as God had said it would. When the man and woman sinned, two things happened. First, they died spiritually, which means that something very important about their relationship with God died. This is why they had to leave the garden. Second, they were doomed to die physically even though they did not die right away. If they had never sinned, they would never have died and never had to leave the garden, just as Christians in heaven will never die and will never have to leave the presence of God.

3. God's mercy was displayed in the garden.
Instead of killing Adam and Eve, God was merciful and gracious. He killed animals and then used their skins to cover Adam and Eve's shameful nakedness. This shedding of animal blood as a substitute punishment for sin was practiced throughout the Old Testament. Every time it happened, it was a picture of how one day Jesus would shed his blood to take our punishment for sin and permanently cover our shame.

Lesson Review

Answer the following statements as True or False:

1. In order to destroy Adam and Eve's relationship with God, Satan disguised himself as a serpent. _____
2. Satan tempted and deceived Adam first. _____
3. Eve ate the fruit and also gave some to Adam. _____
4. When Adam and Eve sinned, they were immediately separated from God. _____
5. Adam and Eve were no longer afraid of God after eating the forbidden fruit. _____

Values for Life

Satan is the same today as he was back then. He is God's enemy and our enemy. He does not want us to listen to God's Word and will use any means to hinder us from doing so. God always does what He says. God doesn't threaten to punish sin and then not do it. He hates everything that is evil and punishes all disobedience to His commands.

Life Response/My Decision

1. I will remember that I was born a sinner because of the original sin of Adam and Eve.
2. I will remember that God's laws are meant to be obeyed and are for the good of His people.
3. I will remember that when I do sin, I need to ask for forgiveness.
4. I will remember that my sins were washed away because of the sacrifices of Jesus.

Activities

Review the words of Satan in Genesis 3:1, 4–5. List all the parts of Satan's words that were true and then list the parts that were lies.

Read Genesis 3:8–13. When God questioned Adam and Eve, what excuses did they make?

This activity is to show you how subtle and sneaky sin can be. The lies of Satan can often be mixed with the truth. Also, when we are caught in sin, we make excuses to protect ourselves.

What other ways can you think of where sin can be masked with truth?

Here are a couple of examples:

1. A cookie that is stolen from a cookie jar will taste good. (The cookie will taste good, but taking it is still wrong.)   2. Hitting your brother after he hits you first it's okay because you didn't start the fight. Hitting a brother is not okay even if you didn't start the hitting. God's word tells us we should not repay evil for evil [1 Peter 3:9].)

Lesson 1: Adam and Eve Disobey God

Memory Verse

All have sinned and fall short of the glory of God. Romans 3:23

Lesson 2: Offering of Cain and Abel

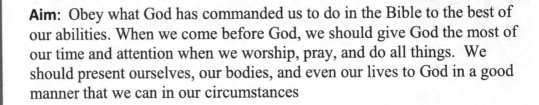

Our disobedience can separate us from God.

Aim: Obey what God has commanded us to do in the Bible to the best of our abilities. When we come before God, we should give God the most of our time and attention when we worship, pray, and do all things. We should present ourselves, our bodies, and even our lives to God in a good manner that we can in our circumstances

Opening Prayer: Dear God, Thank you for blessing us with so much and for giving us the Bible to learn from you. Help us to remember that when we do anything for you God, we should do our best. When we come to church to worship you, help us to be obedient to you and help others and love others to the best of our abilities. Thank you for loving us so much. Amen.

Let's Read more about the story from the Bible!
Genesis 4:3-7
3 In the course of time Cain brought some of the fruits of the soil as an offering to the LORD. 4 And Abel also brought an offering—fat portions from some of the firstborn of his flock. The LORD looked with favor on Abel and his offering, 5 but on Cain and his offering he did not look with favor. So Cain was very angry, and his face was downcast. 6 Then the LORD said to Cain, "Why are you angry? Why is your face downcast? 7 If you do what is right, will you not be accepted? But if you do not do what is right, sin is crouching at your door; it desires to have you, but you must rule over it."

Things to Remember: Main Ideas from the Lesson
God loved both Cain and Abel. Just as God loved Cain and Abel, He also loves us no matter what we look like or our talents. God loves us just the way we are. He wants to have a relationship with us each and every day.

Both Cain and Abel brought an offering to God. Cain and Abel obeyed God by bringing an offering to God. Obedience is very important in Christian life. The Bible helps us understand how we should live our life and we should obey what God tell us just as Cain and Abel obeyed by bringing offerings as God requested.

Abel brought the best of the animal sacrifice to God as he was told, but Cain did not obey God and brought regular fruit and not the first of the fruits or the best to God. Sometimes in life, we do things, but not with our whole life. God wants our best and for us to do things with our whole heart. We are sometimes like Cain and we get lazy or don't obey our parents because we want to do what we want to. When we have this kind of attitude, it is not bringing God our best. We are encouraged to be more like Abel and to bring our best to help others and to let others know about God.

When we do something for God, we should do it to the best of our abilities. In our school for learning and in our house to help our parents and obey them and even in our churches, it is important to give God our best and all of our abilities, gifts, and talents. We should share these with God and God's children.

Lesson Review

1. Cain and Abel were asked to bring the best of their work to God as an _____.

2. Abel brought the best firstborn _____ to God and obeyed what God asked him to do.

3. Cain unfortunately had a bad attitude and did not bring God the best of his _____ and God was not happy.

4. We should _____ God and do everything in our life to the best of our abilities so that God is glorified.

Values for Life

God loves each of us so much and we should offer ourselves to Him in the best way we can. We can do this by worshipping him, singing Christian songs to Him, and even helping and loving others. We must not grumble, but do things to the best of our ability for God. When we are children of God others will see God's love in us and they will come to know God also!

Life Response/My Decision

I will try my best to give God my best in everything that I do!
I will treat everyone fairly and with respect just as I would like to be treated.
I will choose to obey God in every part of my life

Activities

Have a poster board with the words "Our Best" and "Half Effort" with a line down the middle. Use sticky notes with the following scenarios written on them. Next, have the children examine and determine which category the scenario belongs to, and place the notes on the board. Have them do this in a group. Second, give them two sticky notes and have the students write two scenarios from their life when they gave their best effort and half effort.

Scenarios:
- My mom woke me up for church and I quickly got up and got dressed without making my family late.
- While in church worship service, my friend and I played games and whispered loudly to each other.
- My dad gave me $1 for offertory, but I saved it in my pocket so I can buy a piece of candy later that day.
- For Christmas this year I gave away one of my toys that I got as a gift to an orphanage.

- It was Saturday night and I was really tired so I didn't memorize my memory verse and told my teacher I learned the wrong memory verse.

Feel free to add more of your own scenarios for your students to go through. At the end, review with the students how we could change the "Half Effort" scenarios into "Our Best". Discuss why this is so important to God.

Student's, write down what you see on the board down below as a reminder to you.

Lesson 2: Offering of Cain and Abel

Memory Verse
Make every effort to live in peace with everyone and to be holy; without holiness no one will see the Lord.
Hebrews 12:14

Lesson 13: A New Beginning

Aim: God is our Hope and we should worship Him.

Opening Prayer: Dear Heavenly Father, we thank you for this day and for letting us learn about your servant Noah. We thank you for promising to be with us always. We ask that you help us trust and place our hope in You and that Your will be done in our lives. We love you, Amen.

Let's Read more about the story from the Bible!
Genesis 8:13-22

13 By the first day of the first month of Noah's six hundred and first year, the water had dried up from the earth. Noah then removed the covering from the ark and saw that the surface of the ground was dry. 14 By the twenty-seventh day of the second month the earth was completely dry. 15 Then God said to Noah, 16 "Come out of the ark, you and your wife and your sons and their wives. 17 Bring out every kind of living creature that is with you—the birds, the animals, and all the creatures that move along the ground—so they can multiply on the earth and be fruitful and increase in number on it." 18 So Noah came out, together with his sons and his wife and his sons' wives. 19 All the animals and all the creatures that move along the ground and all the birds— everything that moves on land—came out of the ark, one kind after another. 20 Then Noah built an altar to the LORD and, taking some of all the clean animals and clean birds, he sacrificed burnt offerings on it. 21 The LORD smelled the pleasing aroma and said in his heart: "Never again will I curse the ground because of humans, even though every inclination of the human heart is evil from childhood. And never again will I destroy all living creatures, as I have done. 22 "As long as the earth endures, seedtime and harvest, cold and heat, summer and winter, day and night will never cease."

Student Introduction

Do you know what an altar is? Why does our church have an altar? There is nothing magical about this wood, carpet, or steps. But it isn't just any place. This is where we as Christians can come and bring our problems to God as we pray with our Achen and other members of our congregation. It is as if we are laying our problems on the altar to give it completely to God. This place is also where we, as Christians can come and dedicate or make promises to God, and also come to ask for forgiveness of our sins. In today's lesson, we will learn why Noah built an altar to God.

Things to Remember: Main Ideas from the Lesson

We all know the story of Noah and the ark. Noah had his hope in God and knew God would protect him, his family, and the animals in the ark. Noah's hope in God continued when it rained 40 days and 40 nights. Finally, in Genesis 8:13-14, the flood ended and the water had completely dried up from the earth. Let's see what Noah does when God instructs him to finally come out of the ark. Dry land! In Genesis 8:15-17, Noah listened as God instructed him to have everyone and everything come out of the ark. They were all safe and on dry land! What do you think Noah did after all those days in the ark? What would you have done if you finally got off the ark? Maybe jump up and down for joy? A Celebration! In Genesis 8:18-20, the Bible tells us what Noah did. He first obeyed God and got everything out of the ark. After leaving the ark, Noah then built an altar and offered burnt offerings. By doing this, he was praising God, accepting that they were all saved from the flood because of their faith in God. From the very beginning, Noah made a choice to put his hope in God and that God would bring all of them to safety. And God did exactly that! God's Promise! In Genesis 8:21-22, the Bible tells us that God was very pleased with Noah when He saw the altar and the offerings. Noah made God very happy! God promised Noah that He would never curse the ground again because of man and that He would not destroy any living creature with water as He had just done in the flood.

Jesus is our Perfect Sacrifice! Noah honored God by building the altar to worship Him. During the Old Testament times, people used the altar to worship and bring an offering to God. The offering was shedding the blood of an animal. Does anyone notice an animal on our church altar every Sunday? So, why do we not do this today? This is because Jesus is our perfect sacrifice. Jesus came into this world and died on the cross and shed His blood for all of our sins! He did this because He loved us so much. We don't have to build an altar and offer up a dead animal anymore! As Christians, our desire should be to please God with our worship of Him and to always thank Him for sending us the greatest sacrifice, Jesus Christ. Do you come to church just to see your friends? Or do you come to church to worship and learn about God?

Lesson Review

After leaving the ark, Noah praised God.

Noah made a choice to put all his hope in God and God blessed him.

God was happy because Noah trusted in Him and gave thanks.

How can you make God happy like Noah did?

Do you have a special place in your home where you can go and pray or read the Bible?

Values for Life

We have the choice to make God happy or to make Him sad. Sometimes this may not feel like an easy choice but we should remember how God always provides for our needs and how much we need to thank Him for.

Life Response/My Decision

Do you put your hope and trust in God or in something else to make you happy?
If I asked you fill in this sentence, what would you say? I put my hope in God

because_____.

It is important to know why you put your hope in God. It's not because your Sunday school teacher or achen told you to. We know from Noah's story and other stories in the Bible that God can be trusted. God knows every situation that happens in our lives, whether it is at home, school, or with friends. As we put our hope in God, it is not so God will do what we want, but so that He will do what is best for us.

Activities

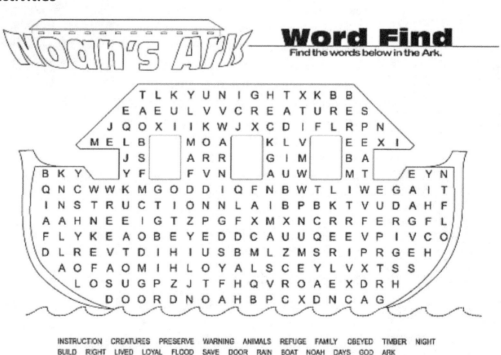

Word Find
Find the words below in the Ark.

INSTRUCTION CREATURES PRESERVE WARNING ANIMALS REFUGE FAMILY OBEYED TIMBER NIGHT
BUILD RIGHT LIVED LOYAL FLOOD SAVE DOOR RAIN BOAT NOAH DAYS GOD ARK

Memory Verse

As long as the earth endures, seed time and harvest, cold and heat, summer and winter, day and night, shall not cease.
Genesis 8:22

9

Lesson 4: The Tower of Babel

Aim: We must realize the consequences of forgetting God's grace and concentrating on one's own achievements. Nothing to boast on our ability, but it is God's gift.

Opening Prayer: Dear God, help us to remember everything we have is a blessing from you. Help us not to be prideful, but to remain humble in all things. Amen

Let's Read more about the story from the Bible!
Genesis 11:1-9

Now the whole world had one language and a common speech. 2 As people moved eastward, they found a plain in Shinar and settled there. 3 They said to each other, "Come, let's make bricks and bake them thoroughly." They used brick instead of stone, and tar for mortar. 4 Then they said, "Come, let us build ourselves a city, with a tower that reaches to the heavens, so that we may make a name for ourselves; otherwise we will be scattered over the face of the whole earth." 5 But the LORD came down to see the city and the tower the people were building. 6 The LORD said, "If as one people speaking the same language they have begun to do this, then nothing they plan to do will be impossible for them. 7 Come, let us go down and confuse their language so they will not understand each other." 8 So the LORD scattered them from there over all the earth, and they stopped building the city. 9 That is why it was called Babel—because there the LORD confused the language of the whole world. From there the LORD scattered them over the face of the whole earth.

Student Introduction

There are many times in our lives that we are very happy and proud of the things we do. Getting good grades, making a beautiful artwork in class, or even just winning a game. We may even show off our house, clothes, or the video games we have at home. We sometimes are very quick to say "I did it!" or we are quick to show off everything that we have and take all the credit for all that we have in life. Its very easy to do and many of us do this, but when we start to look at what we do, we forget all that God has done. When we think of ourselves greater than someone else or even God, that is called pride. Pride can be harmful to us because when we are prideful, we forget to give God credit and we all know that He is the reason we have everything in our life. Just like us many time in our lives, the story we read today is about a group of people who took pride in their strengths and forgot about God. When we do this, it does not make God happy.

Things to Remember: Main Ideas from the Lesson

There was just one language during this time, so everyone one on earth spoke and understood each other very easily. The people could have used this in a good way, but instead the people wanted to make a tower up to the heavens to make a name for themselves (show off to everyone). God was not pleased that they were building the tower to glorify themselves because it is not good to boast about yourself when God is the one that gives us the strength to do everything. The glory should have been for God. God put an end to the tower building by making them to speak different languages so they couldn't communicate and scattered them all over the earth. That is why it is called the Tower of "Babel" because God changed all of their languages and they did not understand each other.

Lesson Review

1. Why is the tower called Babel?

2. What did the people hope to accomplish by building the tower?

3. Why is pride not a good quality in a Christian?

Values for Life

Remain humble in all things and remember that everything we have is because of God.

Life Response/My Decision

Do you put your hope and trust in God or in something else to make you happy? Grace of God is enough.
- Remain humble in everything.
- Use our talents to glorify God and not ourselves.

Activities

- Tower building competition (using cups or marshmallows and toothpicks) Try to build a tower without talking to show how difficult it is to accomplish things without being able to communicate
- Write down on an index card what pride means to you and then discuss you're your classmates what you wrote.

What Did You Say?

```
P R C S K I K T L E B A B E L
Q O S K E W O J A X F Y G U H
E G Q S E W N D O B X A E C T
D X X L E Y K K U N U T N I L
N I M R O D K U I G M Q O N G
V R O Y M U T Y N V W H I A V
M L N O D S L A E N R Q S S M
H E B D P P L X W L K X U H X
E U O V D C K Y B V D H F I U
R G N Y N O X T A V Y C N N K
Y Y E T R H B I M H E I O A G
K R H A E O J C H G U X C R X
A M A K F R L X W O V F B F P
B F Y A D B C G J S T A C K F
H O H A S V E N B V I U I V C
```

BABEL
CITY
CONFUSION
GLORY
GOD
HUNTER
LANGUAGE
NIMROD
SHINAR
TOWER

Memory Verse

For it is by grace you have been saved, through faith—and this is not from yourselves, it is the gift of God- Ephesians 2:8

Lesson 5: God's Special Plan for Children

Each of us has a God given purpose and we are valued in God's eyes.

Aim: God cares for our thoughts and actions, not our outward appearance and we should not judge people either.

Opening Prayer: Dear God, Thank you for creating us all different from each other – from how we look to how we sound. Help us to understand that you care about our loving hearts and desire to serve you instead of first impressions. Let us look at our friends and others we do not know in the way you want us to. We want to live a life that makes You happy. Amen.

Do you know someone who has been singled out from others because of how they look/talk/have a disability or have ever been excluded because of their appearance/disability? How do you think that made them feel?

The focus of this lesson is to show that no matter the outward appearance, God cares for our hearts and intentions — not how nicely we dress or the friends we hang out with. God cares that we treat each other fairly and with love.

Let's Read more about the story from the Bible!
1 Samuel 16:1-13

The LORD said to Samuel, "How long will you grieve over Saul? I have rejected him from being king over Israel. Fill your horn with oil and set out; I will send you to Jesse the Bethlehemite, for I have provided for myself a king among his sons." 2 Samuel said, "How can I go? If Saul hears of it, he will kill me." And the LORD said, "Take a heifer with you, and say, 'I have come to sacrifice to the LORD.'3 Invite Jesse to the sacrifice, and I will show you what you shall do; and you shall anoint for me the one whom I name to you." 4 Samuel did what the LORD commanded, and came to Bethlehem. The elders of the city came to meet him trembling, and said, "Do you come peaceably?" 5 He said, "Peaceably; I have come to sacrifice to the LORD;

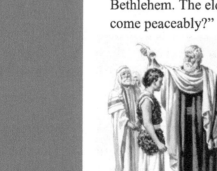

sanctify yourselves and come with me to the sacrifice." And he sanctified Jesse and his sons and invited them to the sacrifice. 6 When they came, he looked on Eliab and thought, "Surely the LORD's anointed is now before the LORD." 7 But the LORD said to Samuel, "Do not look on his appearance or on the height of his stature, because I have rejected him; for the LORD does not see as mortals see; they look on the outward appearance, but the LORD looks on the heart." 8 Then Jesse called Abinadab, and made him pass before Samuel. He said, "Neither has the LORD chosen this one." 9 Then Jesse made Shammah pass by. And he said, "Neither has the LORD chosen this one."

10 Jesse made seven of his sons pass before Samuel, and Samuel said to Jesse, "The LORD has not chosen any of these." 11 Samuel said to Jesse, "Are all your sons here?" And he said, "There remains yet the youngest, but he is keeping the sheep." And Samuel said to Jesse, "Send and bring him; for we will not sit down until he comes here." 12 He sent and brought him in. Now he was ruddy, and had beautiful eyes, and was handsome. The LORD said, "Rise and anoint him; for this is the one." 13 Then Samuel took the horn of oil, and anointed him in the presence of his brothers; and the spirit of the LORD came mightily upon David from that day forward. Samuel then set out and went to Ramah.

Student Introduction

Mother Teresa entire life was fully devoted to helping the poor, the sick, the needy, and the helpless.

Where did Mother Teresa grow up? Mother Teresa was born in Uskub, Ottoman Empire on August 26, 1910. This city is now called Skopje and is the capital of the Republic of Macedonia. Her birth name was Agnes Gonxha Bojaxhiu. Her father died when she was eight and she was raised by her mother. She was raised as a Roman Catholic and decided to devote her life to God at a young age. She joined the Sisters of Loreto at the age of 18 to become a missionary to India. She started her missionary work in Darjeeling, India. She learned the local language, Bengali, and taught at the local school. She soon took her first vows as a nun and took the name Teresa. She would teach for many years in India becoming the headmistress at a school in eastern Calcutta.

What did Mother Teresa do? When she was 36 years old she felt the call from God to help the poor of India. She received some basic medical training and then set out to help the sick and needy. This wasn't an easy task in 1948 India. She had very little support and, while trying to feed and help the poorest of the poor, she herself was constantly hungry and even had to beg for food. Soon other women joined her and she formed the Missionaries of Charity. Mother Teresa described the purpose of the Missionaries of Charity as an organization to take care of "the hungry, the naked, the homeless, the crippled, the blind, the lepers, all those people who feel unwanted, unloved and uncared for throughout society".

Things to Remember: Main Ideas from the Lesson

God had rejected Saul as king of Israel. God wanted a new leader for the Israelites so the Lord asked Samuel to go to Bethlehem so that he could anoint a new king. Samuel feared that King Saul would kill him if he knew that Samuel was looking for a king to replace Samuel. God told Samuel to tell the people that he was going to offer a sacrifice to the Lord. Samuel was then to invite Jesse to the sacrifice and the Lord would instruct what to do. Samuel did so the Lord instructed him and he met Jesse of Bethlehem and waited for the Lord to point out who should be anointed. Jesse brought seven of his sons before Samuel but the Lord told Samuel that none of them were the chosen one. Samuel asked Jesse if he had other children and Jesse showed him the youngest, David the shepherd boy. David did not like a king. He was young and did not look a king. Samuel was looking for someone who looked like a king but God selected the next king based on his heart. We think we know a person based on how a he/she looks. God looks at something that no one else can see: a person's heart. Do we judge others based on how they look or what they wear? God wants us to treat everyone equally regardless of their skin color, beliefs or ideas. God can use anyone, even a young child. God was more interested in the least likely of Samuel's selection because He knew there was something very special about David.

Lesson Review

1. Who did God reject as King of Israel?

2. Which of Samuel's sons did Samuel finally anoint?

Values for Life

God looks at all the same – regardless of our skin color, hair, height, popularity at school, etc. He is concerned only with your true heart and how you can serve Him.

Life Response/My Decision

- I will try my hardest not to judge others by the way they look / their differences from myself. I will treat everyone fairly and with respect just as I would like to be treated.

Activities

Take time to write a letter to someone that you know or someone you know of, that you have seen get bullied or treated poorly because they are different. What would you say to them?

Memory Verse

For the LORD does not see as mortals see; they look on the outward appearance, but the LORD looks on the heart. 1 Samuel 16:7b

Lesson 6: Abram Rescues Lot

Christian loves means helping others in need.

Aim: Despite Lot being separated from Abraham on his own terms, Abraham goes out of his way to rescue him

Opening Prayer: Dear Lord Heavenly Father, we pray that you allow us to understand what Christian Love truly means as we learn about Abraham rescuing Lot, and how we can rescue others every day. We thank you for our Sunday school and pray we live each day by what we learn in class. Amen!

Let's Read more about the story from the Bible!
Genesis 14:11-16
So the enemy took all the goods of Sodom and Gomorrah, and all their provisions, and went their way; they also took Lot, the son of Abram's brother, who lived in Sodom, and his goods, and departed. Then one who had escaped came and told Abram the Hebrew, who was living by the oaks of Mamre the Amorite, brother of Eshcol and of Aner; these were allies of Abram. When Abram heard that his nephew had been taken captive, he led forth his trained men, born in his house, three hundred eighteen of them, and went in pursuit as far as Dan. He divided his forces against them by night, he and his servants, and routed them and pursued them to Hobah, north of Damascus. Then he brought back all the goods, and also brought back his nephew Lot with his goods, and the women and the people.

Draw a picture of Abram rescuing Lot:

Things to Remember: Main Ideas from the Lesson

- Abraham and his nephew Lot lived in different cities because that is what Lot wanted
- Lot was taken captive while living in Sodom
- When Abram heard this, he gathered a small army and rescued Lot, his family, and his possessions
- When the King of Sodom told Abram to just give back all the people he had captured and to keep everything else, Abram refused to take anything for himself.
- Abraham's only concern was that Lot and his family were safe. He did not want any personal glory for himself.

Lesson Review

1. What does it mean to be rescued? By whom in everyday life are we saved by?

2. Name examples of how we can rescue others in our daily lives.

3. Would you say you are saved? If so how did you get there?

Values for Life

- Being "saved" makes a difference in our life.
- It is important for us to help those who are in need.
- Serving others first, despite pride.

Life Response/My Decision

1. Decision is to be saved, and how it changes your life in all aspects.
2. Open up class time for Testimony or discussion in regards to the lesson. (5min)

Memory Verse

Those who say, "I love God," and hate their brothers or sisters, are liars; for those who do not love a brother or sister whom they have seen, cannot love God whom they have not seen. -1 John 4:20

Draw a picture of how God saved you.

Draw a picture how you can help someone in need.

Lesson 7: Aaron and Moses

God chooses and uses us despite our weaknesses.

Aim: God strengthens the meek and uses all kinds of people for His ministry. In the same way God strengthens us, His people, even if we think we are too weak to carry out His will.

Opening Prayer: Dear Lord Heavenly Father, help use to learn about Aaron and Moses and help us to allow you to use in the way you need us like Aaron and Moses was willing. We thank you for our Sunday school and pray we live each day by what we learn in class. Amen!

Let's Read more about the story from the Bible!
Exodus 6:28-7:6 Now when the LORD spoke to Moses in Egypt, he said to him, "I am the LORD. Tell Pharaoh king of Egypt everything I tell you." But Moses said to the LORD, "Since I speak with faltering lips, why would Pharaoh listen to me?" Then the LORD said to Moses, "See, I have made you like God to Pharaoh, and your brother Aaron will be your prophet. You are to say everything I command you, and your brother Aaron is to tell Pharaoh to let the Israelites go out of his country. But I will harden Pharaoh's heart, and though I multiply my signs and wonders in Egypt, he will not listen to you. Then I will lay my hand on Egypt and with mighty acts of judgment I will bring out my divisions, my people the Israelites. And the Egyptians will know that I am the LORD when I stretch out my hand against Egypt and bring the Israelites out of it." Moses and Aaron did just as the LORD commanded them.

> Sometimes we might not feel like we are talented enough or big enough to make a difference for God. Moses is a great example to us that even despite our weakness God can use us to make a difference in this world. You just have to be willing to serve and obey God!

Things to Remember: Main Ideas from the Lesson

1. *We need to have a personal relationship with God* - The number one thing God wants to do with each one of us is to establish a close and personal relationship with Him. Moses definitely accomplished this with God the Father! He entered and followed God's personal call on His life.

2. *God will lead you on a daily basis.* - We see God commanding Moses on how to lead the fight against Pharaoh with step by step instructions. God will also lead you on a daily basis as to what needs to be accomplished in your life. All you have to do is be willing to step into God's plan for your life, and He will then start to take complete control and lead you down the path that He wants you to travel on.

3. *God uses ordinary people who obey Him to accomplish His purpose.* - We see that God has chosen Aaron to be the voice of Moses and to stand up against Pharaoh. Many of us may find ourselves in similar situations someday. We may be asked to do unbelievable things at the direction of God. Moses and Aaron provide the perfect example to us of what God requires--faith, submission and obedience.

Lesson Review

Answer the following statements as True or False:

1. Moses felt he was a confident speaker and could speak to Pharaoh on his own. _____

2. Aaron was acting like a prophet of Moses. _____

3. God hardened Pharaoh's heart. _____

4. Pharaoh listened to Aaron and Moses immediately when they asked to let the Israelites go. _____

5. Aaron and Moses did as the Lord commanded them. _____

Values for Life

1. The Bible says that we are to be led by the Holy Spirit in this life. God perfectly led Moses every step of the way the minute he decided to accept God's call on his life. Christians need to realize that if God calls you to do anything on His behalf, that He will also anoint you with His supernatural power to get the job done. All Christian believers have the Holy Spirit living and dwelling inside of them.

2. Moses was an excellent representative for God. He stayed true, loyal, and faithful to the Lord during difficult times, and he never once strayed from God as His loyal representative. In the same way, God can also use you in a mighty way when the time is right. The Bible says that we are to be ambassadors for Christ. We are His representatives.

Life Response/My Decision

1. I will remember that even though I am an ordinary person by this world's standards, I can be used for extraordinary purposes to fulfill God's will.
2. I will remind myself that I should be obedient and constantly listening for God's call.
3. I will remember that despite my weaknesses, God will strengthen me for His needs.
4. I will remind myself that I need to continually work as God's hands and feet, to help spread the Gospel message here on earth.

Moses and Aaron Word Search

Y	I	H	F	B	P	Q	H	J	O
K	S	G	X	T	H	Z	I	I	A
G	R	O	C	C	A	A	X	T	Z
R	A	D	P	M	R	C	H	M	T
C	E	M	U	X	A	A	F	E	E
A	L	O	Y	F	O	A	H	L	L
L	I	S	P	R	H	P	R	Q	N
L	T	E	E	L	O	D	E	O	S
P	E	S	X	R	J	J	G	C	N
T	S	C	P	P	Q	L	S	L	S

Find the following words in the puzzle:

MOSES

PHARAOH

AARON

ISRAELITES

CALL

GOD

PROPHET

Memory Verse

I can do all this through him who gives me strength.
Philippians 4:13

Lesson 8: God's Helper

God wants to use us to help others and extend His grace and love.

Aim:
- God can use us in many ways to help others
- Consider what you can do to help others and how this can be an expression of your faith
- Make a plan to play a Christian role in humanity by offering a helping hand

Opening Prayer: Dear Lord Heavenly Father, we pray that you allow us to understand what it means to obey you and to help others. Help us to remember that we are a witness to others of Your love and grace. We thank you for our Sunday school and pray we live each day by what we learn in class. Amen!

Let's Read more about the story from the Bible!
Joshua 2:1-18 **Spies Sent to Jericho**

Then Joshua son of Nun sent two men secretly from Shittim as spies, saying, "Go, view the land, especially Jericho." So they went, and entered the house of a prostitute whose name was Rahab, and spent the night there. The king of Jericho was told, "Some Israelites have come here tonight to search out the land." Then the king of Jericho sent orders to Rahab, "Bring out the men who have come to you, who entered your house, for they have come only to search out the whole land." But the woman took the two men and hid them. Then she said, "True, the men came to me, but I did not know where they came from.

And when it was time to close the gate at dark, the men went out. Where the men went I do not know. Pursue them quickly, for you can overtake them." She had, however, brought them up to the roof and hidden them with the stalks of flax that she had laid out on the roof. So the men pursued them on the way to the Jordan as far as the fords. As soon as the pursuers had gone out, the gate was shut. Before they went to sleep, she came up to them on the roof and said to the men: "…Now then, since I have dealt kindly with you, swear to me by the Lord that you in turn will deal kindly with my family. Give me a sign of good faith that you will spare my father and mother, my brothers and sisters, and all who belong to them, and deliver our lives from death." The men said to her, "Our life for yours! If you do not tell this business of ours, then we will deal kindly and faithfully with you when the Lord gives us the land."

Things to Remember: Main Ideas from the Lesson

1. God did not hesitate to use a person with a sinful life to help others. We are each capable of sharing God's love and helping others; no person is incapable of great things with God by their side.
2. Even though Rahab had lived a sinful life, she decided to change when she heard about the amazing things God had done.
3. Our focus is on the faith Rahab had and how she helped to fulfill God's will by saving the lives of the two spies.
4. Rahab and her family were saved and were shown kindness because of her faith (unity) and the help she offered to God's people.

Lesson Review

1. What was the name of the city where Joshua sent two spies?

2. Whose house did the spies stay in?

3. What did Rahab do when the King sent soldiers to arrest the spies?

4. How did the spies get out of Jericho?

Values for Life

- God can use young children like me to do the greatest things!

Life Response/My Decision

- I may be young and small, but I can do many things to help others in need.

Rahab

Rahab helped two Israelite spies hide and later escape from her house in Jericho.

The following words were taken from Joshua 2. Find and circle them in the word search.

JOSHUA	JORDAN	KING	CORD
NUN	SWEAR	ISRAEL	SCARLET
SENT	LORD	TWO	OATH
SPY	SAVE	GATE	STALKS
JERICHO	HIDE	ROOF	FLAX
RAHAB	WALL		

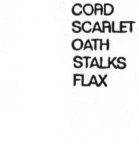

```
S L K I N G B O S I F T
E W O S P Y A J Q O L S
L J E R I C H O O Y A K
L O M A D E A R P V X L
A S S E R T R D E L I A
W H E L H S C A R L E T
N U N E D I H N U S W S
G A T E L L O D R O C I
```

Lesson 8: God's Helper

Lesson 9: Faith in the Fire

Being faithful to God even when things get hard!

Aim: Our God is a mighty God and is always faithful to His people. As Christians we must stand strong in our faith in God and in God's teachings even during difficult times.

Opening Prayer: Dear Lord Heavenly Father, we know that life is not easy at times and sometimes we are faced with hard times. God help us to be faithful to you even during hard times. Help us to know that you are there always. We thank you for our Sunday school and pray we live each day by what we learn in class. Amen!

Let's Read more about the story from the Bible!
Daniel 3: 16-29

Shadrach, Meshach, and Abednego answered the king, "O Nebuchadnezzar, we have no need to present a defense to you in this matter. If our God whom we serve is able to deliver us from the furnace of blazing fire and out of your hand, O king, let him deliver us. But if not, be it known to you, O king, that we will not serve your gods and we will not worship the golden statue that you have set up." Then Nebuchadnezzar was so filled with rage against Shadrach, Meshach, and Abednego that his face was distorted. He ordered the furnace heated up seven times more than was customary, and ordered some of the strongest guards in his army to bind Shadrach, Meshach, and Abednego and to throw them into the furnace of blazing fire. So the men were bound, still wearing their tunics, their trousers, their hats, and their other garments, and they were thrown into the furnace of blazing fire. Because the king's command was urgent and the furnace was so overheated, the raging flames killed the men who lifted Shadrach, Meshach, and Abednego. But the three men, Shadrach, Meshach, and Abednego, fell down, bound, into the furnace of blazing fire.

Then King Nebuchadnezzar was astonished and rose up quickly. He said to his counselors, "Was it not three men that we threw bound into the fire?" They answered the king, "True, O king." He replied, "But I see four men unbound, walking in the middle of the fire, and they are not hurt; and the fourth has the appearance of a god." Nebuchadnezzar then approached the door of the furnace of blazing fire and said, "Shadrach, Meshach, and Abednego, servants of the Most High God, come out! Come here!" So Shadrach, Meshach, and Abednego came out from the fire. And the satraps, the prefects, the governors, and the king's counselors gathered together and saw that the fire had not had any power over the bodies of those men; the hair of their heads was not singed, their tunics were not harmed, and not even the smell of fire came from them. Nebuchadnezzar said, "Blessed be the God of Shadrach, Meshach, and Abednego, who has sent his angel and delivered his servants who trusted in him. They disobeyed the king's command and yielded up their bodies rather than serve and worship any god except their own God. Therefore I make a decree: Any people, nation, or language that utters blasphemy against the God of Shadrach, Meshach, and Abednego shall be torn limb from limb, and their houses laid in ruins; for there is no other god who is able to deliver in this way."

Things to Remember: Main Ideas from the Lesson

1. King Nebuchadnezzar did not follow God's laws.
2. The King tried to make Shadrach, Meshach, and Abednego obey rules that were against God, but they refused to obey.
3. The king was angry and commanded them to be thrown into the fire, but they did not burn up or even smell like smoke!
4. God sent an angel in the fire to protect the three men.
5. The three men remained faithful to God even when they were faced with death in the fire. Their faith was great and an example to us all.

Lesson Review

1. What did Shadrach and his friends refuse to do?

2. How did King Nebuchadnezzar react when he found out that Shadrach, Meshach and Abednego had not worshiped the statue?

3. What made the king surprised when he looked into the fiery furnace?

4. What happened to the soldiers who were putting Shadrach, Meshach and Abednego into the furnace?

5. Who was the fourth man in the furnace with Shadrach, Meshach and Abednego?

6. What lesson about faith do you learn from this story?

Values for Life

1. We can trust God to deliver us. We need to be faithful to serve God in all circumstances whether God helps us or not.
2. Trust God to be with us through any trouble we may face because He has promised us this.
3. It is important to follow God's way always so that when we are tempted to do the wrong things, we can make the right decision to follow God.
4. We should tell others about our faith in God during difficult times so they can see how good God is.

Life Response/My Decision

I will trust God in all circumstances. I will pray and have faith that God is with me even when things are hard and there are many troubles in my life. God will help us and will be with us.

Shadrach, Meshach and Abednego Crossword

Across
2. The three men were _____ because they didn't know if God would save them.
4. Shadrach, Meshach and Abednego wouldn't do this to any other god.
6. Even though the king put three men in the furnace, he saw ____.
8. The king believed that his _____ was real and could hear him.
9. The three men were completely _____ as they came out of the hot furnace.

Down
1. When the music started to play everyone was ordered to do this.
3. God did this so that the men wouldn't burn in the furnace.
5. The name of the place where the story took place.
6. The three men were thrown into a very hot _____ for not bowing to a statue.
7. The three men _____ that God was real and that He listens to them.

Memory Verse

"…but those who wait for the LORD shall renew their strength, they shall mount up with wings like eagles, they shall run and not be weary, they shall walk and not faint." - Isaiah 40:31

Lesson 10: Elisha & the Shunammite Women

God takes care of His people.

Aim: To remember how God takes care of His people in their times of need and will use His people to reach out to those in need.

Opening Prayer: Dear Lord Heavenly Father, help us to have an open heart and mind as we learn today about Elisha and the Shunammite women. Help us to know that you take care of us all the time. We thank you for our Sunday school and pray we live each day by what we learn in class. Amen!

Let's Read more about the story from the Bible!
2 Kings 4:18-36

[18] When the child was older, he went out one day to his father among the reapers. [19] He complained to his father, "Oh, my head, my head!" The father said to his servant, "Carry him to his mother." [20] He carried him and brought him to his mother; the child sat on her lap until noon, and he died. [21] She went up and laid him on the bed of the man of God, closed the door on him, and left. [22] Then she called to her husband, and said, "Send me one of the servants and one of the donkeys, so that I may quickly go to the man of God and come back again." [23] He said, "Why go to him today? It is neither new moon nor sabbath." She said, "It will be all right." [24] Then she saddled the donkey and said to her servant, "Urge the animal on; do not hold back for me unless I tell you." [25] So she set out, and came to the man of God at Mount Carmel.

When the man of God saw her coming, he said to Gehazi his servant, "Look, there is the Shunammite woman; [26] run at once to meet her, and say to her, Are you all right? Is your husband all right? Is the child all right?" She answered, "It is all right." [27] When she came to the man of God at the mountain, she caught hold of his feet. Gehazi approached to push her away. But the man of God said, "Let her alone, for she is in bitter distress; the LORD has hidden it from me and has not told me." [28] Then she said, "Did I ask my lord for a son? Did I not say, Do not mislead me?" [29] He said to Gehazi, "Gird up your loins, and take my staff in your hand, and go. If you meet anyone, give no greeting, and if anyone greets you, do not answer; and lay my staff on the face of the child." [30] Then the mother of the child said, "As the LORD lives, and as you yourself live, I will not leave without you." So he rose up and followed her. [31] Gehazi went on ahead and laid the staff on the face of the child, but there was no sound or sign of life. He came back to meet him and told him, "The child has not awakened."

[32] When Elisha came into the house, he saw the child lying dead on his bed. [33] So he went in and closed the door on the two of them, and prayed to the LORD. [34] Then he got up on the bed and lay upon the child, putting his mouth upon his mouth, his eyes upon

his eyes, and his hands upon his hands; and while he lay bent over him, the flesh of the child became warm. [35] He got down, walked once to and fro in the room, then got up again and bent over him; the child sneezed seven times, and the child opened his eyes. [36] Elisha summoned Gehazi and said, "Call the Shunammite woman." So he called her. When she came to him, he said, "Take your son."

Things to Remember: Main Ideas from the Lesson

1. The Shunammite woman's son died and the woman remembered Elisha, the man of God.
2. The Shunammite woman went searching for Elisha to tell him to help heal her son.
3. Elisha came to help and with God's help, gave life back to the little boy and he was alive again.
4. The Shunammite woman cried for help and Elisha, with God's help was able to heal the boy.
5. God cares for His people and God used Elisha to reach out to the Shunammite woman and her son.

Lesson Review

1. What was Elisha's servant's name?

2. When the boy went out to the field with his father what happened?

3. How did Elisha help the woman?

4. Who showed love in our story today?

5. How did Elisha show God's love?

6. Why do you think it is important to show God's love instead of just talking about it?

Values for Life

- It is important to show kindness to others like the Shunammite woman.
- God will reward those who serve others.
- God hears our cries for help and hears our daily prayers.
- God cares for His people and God will use people to help others.

Life Response/My Decision

I will show kindness to those around me so that I am showing God's love to everyone. If someone is needing help, I will think of ways that I can help them and show them God's love.

Crossword Puzzle about Elisha and the Shunammite Woman

```
N A R Y D S G H A S
B Q H E E E O H L T
A Y A C H K S N B A
L D J A G I N T E F
U H Z Y L Z P O J F
G I Q E X O M R D X
P Q H E A D A C H E
E T I M M A N U H S
W E Z E E N S Q P F
N Y L V A L I V E M
```

ALIVE
DEAD
DONKEY
ELISHA
GEHAZI

HEADACHE
SHUNAMMITE
SNEEZE
SON
STAFF

Memory Verse

"As a father has compassion for his children, so the LORD has compassion for those who fear him." -Psalm 103:13

Lesson 11: God's Glory

God's glory is seen through His creation.

Aim: To remember recognize how good God's creation is and to identify how things that God created glorifies Him and how we should glorify Him through our lives.

Opening Prayer: Dear Lord Heavenly Father, we are so grateful that you have created everything in this world. Help us today to recognize how every day your creation brings your glory just by being. Help us to identify how we can bring you glory and help us to glorify you through our lives every single day. Amen.

Let's Read more about the story from the Bible!
Psalm 19:1-6

[1] The heavens declare the glory of God;
  the skies proclaim the work of his hands.
[2] Day after day they pour forth speech;
  night after night they reveal knowledge.
[3] They have no speech, they use no words;
  no sound is heard from them.
[4] Yet their voice goes out into all the earth,
  their words to the ends of the world.
In the heavens God has pitched a tent for the sun.
[5] It is like a bridegroom coming out of his chamber,
  like a champion rejoicing to run his course.
[6] It rises at one end of the heavens
  and makes its circuit to the other;
  nothing is deprived of its warmth.

Psalm 19 can be considered to be a hymn of thanksgiving and praising God because He is God. **This psalm looks at God's creations and** *highlights how creation glorifies its Creator.*

Things to Remember: Main Ideas from the Lesson

1. Everything that God created brings Him glory.
2. These created things have no speech or words, but they still bring Him glory through the way they are.
3. Everything on earth brings God glory from east to west.
4. Just like the creation brings God glory, it is important that we also bring God glory.

Lesson Review

1. The heaven's declare God's _____.

2. The heavens and skies have no _____, use no _____, and

   no _____ is heard from them, but they still bring God glory.

3. Their voices goes out into all of the _____ and their words

   to the _____ of the _____.

4. The _____ is like a bridegroom coming out of his chambers, like a champion rejoicing to run his course.

5. Nothing is deprived from the sun's _____.

Values for Life

- Respect all created things because it brings glory to God.
- Take time to look at all nature and enjoy and view how they glorify God and join them in this through your life every single day.
- Your life should bring God glory just as all created things do.
- Saint Francis of Assisi stated "Preach the gospel at all times, if necessary use words". In the same way, our lives should reflect our faith and should glorify God at all times.

Life Response/My Decision

I will take time to observe nature in my daily life and see how nature glorifies God. I will think of this to remind me that I also should glorify God through my life. I don't necessarily have to use my words or my voice, but my life should glorify God and make Him known to those around me.

Draw a picture of yourself and then around your picture, write down different ways that you glorify God on a daily basis. Then under it, think of ways that you can glorify God (things that you have not done). Draw a candle next to your picture so it is a reminder that you are a light in this darkened world and that when you shine God's light you glorify Him and others are able to see Him through your life.

Memory Verse

"You are worthy, our Lord and God, to receive glory and honor and power, for you created all things, and by your will they were created and have their being." –Revelation 4:11

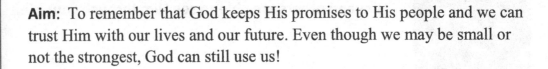

Lesson 12: Gideon and the fleece

God keeps His promise to His people and we can trust Him.

Aim: To remember that God keeps His promises to His people and we can trust Him with our lives and our future. Even though we may be small or not the strongest, God can still use us!

Opening Prayer: Dear Lord Heavenly Father, thank you for being a God who listens to our prayers and still communicates to us. Thank you for loving us the way we are and for wanting to help us and have a relationship with us. Help us to remember that you keep your promises about our life and future. Amen.

Let's Read more about the story from the Bible!
Judges 6: 36-40

[36] Gideon said to God, "If you will save Israel by my hand as you have promised— [37] look, I will place a wool fleece on the threshing floor. If there is dew only on the fleece and all the ground is dry, then I will know that you will save Israel by my hand, as you said." [38] And that is what happened. Gideon rose early the next day; he squeezed the fleece and wrung out the dew—a bowlful of water.

[39] Then Gideon said to God, "Do not be angry with me. Let me make just one more request. Allow me one more test with the fleece, but this time make the fleece dry and let the ground be covered with dew." [40] That night God did so. Only the fleece was dry; all the ground was covered with dew.

Things to Remember: Main Ideas from the Lesson

1. God had promised Gideon that he would be the one to save Israel.
2. Gideon had and personal relationship with God and asked God for a sign to confirm that he would be the one to save Israel.
3. The first morning, the fleece was wet with dew and the ground was dry.
4. The second morning, the fleece was dry and the ground was wet with dew.
5. God was patient with Gideon. Although Gideon didn't have enough faith to believe God the first time, God answers his request again.

Lesson Review

1. What did God promise Gideon?

2. Why would Gideon test God's promise?

3. What did Gideon find the first morning?

4. What did Gideon find on the second morning?

5. What was Gideon's relationship with God?

Values for Life

- When God makes promises about our lives, we should trust Him.
- We can know His promises for our lives through His Word, the Bible.
- We can trust God with our future and that He will take care of us.

Life Response/My Decision

I will trust God and have an personal relationship with God about my own life. If I have questions about my life or my future, I will pray to God about it and wait patiently for His response. I will read the Bible to understand what God's promises are for my life.

CRYPTOGRAM

A	B	C	D	E	F	G	H	I	J	K	L	M	N	O	P	Q	R	S	T	U	V	W	X	Y	Z
4	18	7	6	20	9	16	19	26	15	1	10	8	12	22	17	3	14	25	11	5	23	2	24	13	21

__ __ __ __ __ __   __ __ __ __ __   __ __ __   __ __

16 26 6 20 22 12   4 25 1 20 6   16 22 6   11 22

__ __ __ __ __ __ __   __ __ __   __ __ __ __ __ __ __   __ __ __ __

7 22 12 9 26 14 8   19 26 25   17 14 22 8 26 25 20   2 26 11 19

__ __ __ __ __ __   __ __ __   __ __ __ .

9 10 20 20 7 20   4 12 6   6 20 2

Directions:
This puzzle is called a Cryptogram. I've always loved doing them! At the top there is a KEY that lists all the letters from A thru Z with a box below. Each of the letters has a corresponding number.

The bottom part contains a secret phrase. Each of the blanks has a number underneath it. Fill in the letters that correspond to the numbers below the blanks to solve the phrase.

Memory Verse
"The LORD is faithful in all his words, and gracious in all his deeds."
–Psalm 145:13

36

Lesson 13: Joshua's Decision

We should remember all that God has done for us and serve Him faithfully.

Aim: To remember that God has always been faithful to us and our families and we should live our lives faithfully for Him.

Opening Prayer: Dear Lord Heavenly Father, thank you for being a God who is faithful always. Thank you for being with us through all of our journeys and for keeping us safe and never leaving us. Help us to live lives that are faithful to you and that serve you always. Amen.

Let's Read more about the story from the Bible!
Joshua 24:14-17

¹⁴ "Now fear the LORD and serve him with all faithfulness. Throw away the gods your ancestors worshiped beyond the Euphrates River and in Egypt, and serve the LORD. ¹⁵ But if serving the LORD seems undesirable to you, then choose for yourselves this day whom you will serve, whether the gods your ancestors served beyond the Euphrates, or the gods of the Amorites, in whose land you are living. But as for me and my household, we will serve the LORD."

¹⁶ Then the people answered, "Far be it from us to forsake the LORD to serve other gods! ¹⁷ It was the LORD our God himself who brought us and our parents up out of Egypt, from that land of slavery, and performed those great signs before our eyes. He protected us on our entire journey and among all the nations through which we traveled.

As for me and my house we will serve the LORD

-JOSHUA 24:15

Sometimes when we read books like Joshua we might think that we don't bow down and worship pretend idols so we have nothing to worry about. You and I may never bow down to a little statue but anytime we focus more on anyone or anything more than God we are serving false gods.

Things to Remember: Main Ideas from the Lesson

1. We must be faithful to God by serving him and honoring him.
2. We must choose who we will serve. We cannot serve the things of this world and God. We have to choose.
3. God has been faithful to His people and it was important for the Israelites to remember that.

Lesson Review

1. What are some things that the Lord did for the Israelites that they remembered in this lesson?

2. What did the Israelites decide to do?

3. What are some things that we worship everyday other than God?

4. What are some ways that we can serve God?

Values for Life

- It is important for us to this about our lives and remember what God has done for us and how faithful He has been even when things are/were hard.
- We must make a decision to serve the Lord and renew this commitment every single day.

Life Response/My Decision

I will remember all the things that God has done for me. He has been faithful to me and my family through the good times and the bad times. Because God loves us so much, I will choose to serve the Lord for who He is and because He loves me and my family the way He does.

***Draw things in this world that we worship every day and we don't really think about it. Write next to it, ways that we can turn those things around to be serving God.

Memory Verse

But as for me and my household, we will serve the LORD.

-Joshua 24:15

Lesson 14: David Spares Saul

God does not want us to hold grudges or do acts of revenge.

Aim: To remember that we do not have to take revenge or be hurtful to others because of wrongs they might have done to us. God will take care of things and we need to do good as God has commanded us.

Opening Prayer: Dear Lord Heavenly Father, there are times in our lives that we might want to take care of things by ourselves, especially if we have troubles in our lives or if we want to take revenge. Please give us the strength to pray for those who might have done wrong to us and to stand strong and love them instead of seeking revenge. Amen.

Let's Read more about the story from the Bible!
1 Samuel 24: 1-13

After Saul returned from pursuing the Philistines, he was told, "David is in the Desert of En Gedi." [2] So Saul took three thousand able young men from all Israel and set out to look for David and his men near the Crags of the Wild Goats.

[3] He came to the sheep pens along the way; a cave was there, and Saul went in to relieve himself. David and his men were far back in the cave. [4] The men said, "This is the day the LORD spoke of when he said to you, 'I will give your enemy into your hands for you to deal with as you wish.'" Then David crept up unnoticed and cut off a corner of Saul's robe.

[5] Afterward, David was conscience-stricken for having cut off a corner of his robe. [6] He said to his men, "The LORD forbid that I should do such a thing to my master, the LORD's anointed, or lay my hand on him; for he is the anointed of the LORD." [7] With these words David sharply rebuked his men and did not allow them to attack Saul. And Saul left the cave and went his way.

[8] Then David went out of the cave and called out to Saul, "My lord the king!" When Saul looked behind him, David bowed down and prostrated himself with his face to the ground. [9] He said to Saul, "Why do you listen when men say, 'David is bent on harming you'? [10] This day you have seen with your own eyes

how the LORD delivered you into my hands in the cave. Some urged me to kill you, but I spared you; I said, 'I will not lay my hand on my lord, because he is the LORD's anointed.' [11] See, my father, look at this piece of your robe in my hand! I cut off the corner of your robe but did not kill you. See that there is nothing in my hand to indicate that I am guilty of wrongdoing or rebellion. I have not wronged you, but you are hunting me down to take my life. [12] May the LORD judge between you and me. And may the LORD avenge the wrongs you have done to me, but my hand will not touch you. [13] As the old saying goes, 'From evildoers come evil deeds,' so my hand will not touch you.

Things to Remember: Main Ideas from the Lesson

1. Saul felt jealous and threatened by David because he felt that David would take over his throne one day.
2. Saul went out to kill David and wanted to take revenge.
3. David saw Saul and had the opportunity to kill Saul, but he only cut his robe.
4. David felt bad that he even did that much.
5. David did not take revenge on Saul even though Saul was coming after him to kill him.

Lesson Review

1. Why was Saul trying to kill David?

2. How did David respond to Saul?

3. When David spared Saul's life, what was Saul's response?

4. What should your response be when tempted to get even?

5. When are you most tempted to "get even?"

6. What is it about those situations give in #5 that upset you?

Values for Life

- Revenge is not in our hands. We should love our neighbors and our enemies and not take revenge into our hands.
- We should love our neighbors and pray for them instead of fighting back. Ask God for strength to endure hard situations in our lives instead of taking matters into our own hands.

Life Response/My Decision

Like David, I will withhold from taking revenge on my neighbors or enemies. I will seek God for problems that I might be facing and ask the Lord to take on the problems instead of me taking revenge.

Word Puzzle

```
D M A L A T J L L X E Z L J A
A J E K U B I L L G V S D B O
V N P N G A I G N B A R O B E
I S V F N K S A V S C E E J Y
D A E V I S R A E L C G S Z Z
T J Q N V E F I N K A A L E X
N I H M I H V Q I R V S R Y H
T K G L G T E Q U E G T L E O
Q H D V R X S O D N P D H U D
T E Z S O M C I X I C B A R D
Z O E L F Z Z W L X H F C L A
H I Y F V T V N F I O K U S M
V I V D E V E C R G H G B L F
U D D M E P D R D O Y P H Q L
N A D C K G C N O U O U V Z G
```

CAVE
COURAGE
DAVID
FORGIVING
ISRAEL
KILL
KNIFE
MEN
PHILISTINES
ROBE
SAUL
SAVED
SCARED

Memory Verse
"Do not seek revenge or bear a grudge against one of your people, but love your neighbor has yourself."
–Leviticus 19:18

Lesson 15: Writing on the Wall

We should tell the truth even when it is difficult to do.

Aim: To remember to obey God and telling the truth is very important for our lives. We must be honest with ourselves and others in order to live a life that is pleasing to God.

Opening Prayer: Dear Lord Heavenly Father, please give us the strength to be honest with our everyday lives. There are times in our lives that we are tempted to lie, steal, or be dishonest, but please remind us that doing such things is not pleasing to you. Help us to live a life that is honoring you and honest to all. Amen.

Let's Read more about the story from the Bible!
Daniel 5:1-7, 13, 26-27

King Belshazzar gave a great banquet for a thousand of his nobles and drank wine with them. [2] While Belshazzar was drinking his wine, he gave orders to bring in the gold and silver goblets that Nebuchadnezzar his father had taken from the temple in Jerusalem, so that the king and his nobles, his wives and his concubines might drink from them. [3] So they brought in the gold goblets that had been taken from the temple of God in Jerusalem, and the king and his nobles, his wives and his concubines drank from them. [4] As they drank the wine, they praised the gods of gold and silver, of bronze, iron, wood and stone.

[5] Suddenly the fingers of a human hand appeared and wrote on the plaster of the wall, near the lampstand in the royal palace. The king watched the hand as it wrote. [6] His face turned pale and he was so frightened that his legs became weak and his knees were knocking.

[7] The king summoned the enchanters, astrologers and diviners. Then he said to these wise men of Babylon, "Whoever reads this writing and tells me what it means will be clothed in purple and have a gold chain placed around his neck, and he will be made the third highest ruler in the kingdom."

Verse 13 So Daniel was brought before the king.
And Daniel read the writings on the wall:

26 "Here is what these words mean:
Mene: God has numbered the days of your reign and brought it to an end.
27 *Tekel*: You have been weighed on the scales and found wanting.
28 *Peres*: Your kingdom is divided and given to the Medes and Persians."

Main Ideas from the Lesson

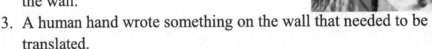

1. Belshazzar knew that the goblets were stolen from the temple, but still used them for his extravagant banquet.
2. Belshazzar's boasting in something that was stolen was exposed by the writing on the wall.
3. A human hand wrote something on the wall that needed to be translated.
4. Daniel was chosen to translate the words.
5. Belshazzar's days were to come to an end because of his wrong doings.

Lesson Review: True or False

— Belshazzar gave orders to bring in the gold and silver goblets that Nebuchadnezzar his father had taken from the temple in Jerusalem

— Belshazzar honored God by keeping the goblet's safe.

— Belshazzar saw human fingers writing a message on the wall.

— Belshazzar was excited for the writing on the wall!

— Daniel came to help translate what the writing on the wall was.

— One part of the writing on the wall said "God has numbered the days of your reign and brought it to an end."

Values for Life
1. It is important to be honest in our lives because it is pleasing to God.
2. Sometimes it is hard for us to be honest because things would be easier if we just kept a lie, but God teaches us to be honest.

3. There are consequences for our dishonesty or lies, so it is better for us to be truthful in everything, even if it is hard to do.

Life Response/My Decision

I will be honest with things in my life even when it becomes difficult. I will pray that God will give me the strength and wisdom to do what is right so that my life is pleasing to God even if it is sometimes not what everyone else is doing or wanting me to do.

THE WRITING ON THE WALL WORD SEARCH

```
I  B  K  Y  B  A  R  Z  L  E  K  E  T  H  L
A  N  E  B  V  U  K  H  V  Q  K  T  U  X  U
A  H  T  L  L  E  G  K  C  N  W  S  T  O  W
U  T  I  E  S  G  S  K  C  Y  L  A  R  I  Q
E  T  S  N  R  H  H  S  H  M  W  E  O  R  N
N  R  E  O  P  P  A  S  E  A  W  F  U  F  I
Q  R  P  I  P  M  R  Z  D  L  Z  W  B  Y  S
P  W  W  T  Y  W  E  E  Z  O  S  U  L  P  U
N  P  R  P  F  A  S  N  T  A  G  N  E  D  P
A  N  I  I  O  F  G  R  E  A  R  U  D  F  H
Y  K  T  R  J  W  D  R  E  S  T  A  F  B  A
Q  B  I  C  W  T  V  E  R  G  N  I  L  E  R
U  C  N  S  S  O  B  N  E  I  N  D  O  H  S
Q  D  G  N  S  M  G  C  E  V  O  I  Y  N  I
T  W  I  I  I  J  C  L  M  Y  A  L  F  T  N
```

Find the following words:
BELSHAZZAR
GODS RULES
UPHARSIN DANIEL
INSCRIPTION
TEKEL
VESSELS
FEAST
INTERPRETATION
TROUBLED WRITING
FINGERS
MENE

Memory Verse

Even a child is known by his actions, by whether his conduct is pure and right.

Proverbs 20:11

Lesson 16: Birth of John the Baptist

God has the power to do amazing things!

Aim: To remember that our God is still a God that does amazing things in our lives. The fact that we have life and many blessings is amazing and we should give thanks to God for loving us in the ways that He does.

Opening Prayer: Dear Lord Heavenly Father, we thank you Father that you are a God that does amazing things in our lives. Even when the world says that it is impossible, through you it is possible. Help us to have solid faith in Your ways and to firmly believe that you are faithful and that you hear our prayers. Amen.

Let's Read more about the story from the Bible!
Luke 1:5-25

5 In the time of Herod king of Judea there was a priest named Zechariah, who belonged to the priestly division of Abijah; his wife Elizabeth was also a descendant of Aaron. 6 Both of them were righteous in the sight of God, observing all the Lord's commands and decrees blamelessly. 7 But they were childless because Elizabeth was not able to conceive, and they were both very old.

8 Once when Zechariah's division was on duty and he was serving as priest before God, 9 he was chosen by lot, according to the custom of the priesthood, to go into the temple of the Lord and burn incense. 10 And when the time for the burning of incense came, all the assembled worshipers were praying outside.

11 Then an angel of the Lord appeared to him, standing at the right side of the altar of incense. 12 When Zechariah saw him, he was startled and was gripped with fear. 13 But the angel said to him: "Do not be afraid, Zechariah; your prayer has been heard. Your wife Elizabeth will bear you a son, and you are to call him John. 14 He will be a joy and delight to you, and many will rejoice because of his birth, 15 for he will be great in the sight of the Lord. He is never to take wine or other fermented drink, and he will be filled with the Holy Spirit even before he is born. 16 He will bring back many of the people of Israel to the Lord their God. 17 And he will go on before the Lord, in the spirit and power of Elijah, to turn the hearts of

46

the parents to their children and the disobedient to the wisdom of the righteous—to make ready a people prepared for the Lord."

¹⁸ Zechariah asked the angel, "How can I be sure of this? I am an old man and my wife is well along in years."

¹⁹ The angel said to him, "I am Gabriel. I stand in the presence of God, and I have been sent to speak to you and to tell you this good news. ²⁰ And now you will be silent and not able to speak until the day this happens, because you did not believe my words, which will come true at their appointed time."

²¹ Meanwhile, the people were waiting for Zechariah and wondering why he stayed so long in the temple. ²² When he came out, he could not speak to them. They realized he had seen a vision in the temple, for he kept making signs to them but remained unable to speak.

²³ When his time of service was completed, he returned home. ²⁴ After this his wife Elizabeth became pregnant and for five months remained in seclusion. ²⁵ "The Lord has done this for me," she said. "In these days he has shown his favor and taken away my disgrace among the people."

Main Ideas from the Lesson
• Zechariah and Elizabeth were wanting to have a child, but they were very old.
• The angel of the Lord appeared to Zechariah and gave him good news that Elizabeth will have a child that will be called John.
• Because Zechariah did not believe the angel's message, he was mute until the birth of John.

Lesson Review (circle the right answer):
1. Zechariah was a (king, priest, baker).
2. Zechariah and Elizabeth thought they were too (young, old, poor) to have a baby.
3. The angel told Zechariah to name the baby (Zacharias, Jesus, John).
4. God took away Zechariah voice because Zechariah (doubted God, got angry at God, believed God).

5. John's important job was to (rule people, raise animals, tell people about Jesus).

6. God always (keeps, breaks, forgets) His promises.

Values for Life

1. In life, God has a perfect time for everything. Sometimes we have plans and times we want to do things, but God is ultimately in control and will do amazing things.

2. We must believe that what is impossible for man is possible with God.

3. We can keep our hope and trust in God and pray for His perfect timing in our lives.

Life Response/My Decision

1. I will keep my trust and hope in God.

2. I will wait patiently for God.

3. I will remember that with God all things are possible.

4. I will believe that our God still does amazing things in our lives.

GABRIEL'S MESSAGE

Unscramble the letters in this message
to find out what the angel Gabriel told Zechariah.

"Do not be _ _ _ _ _, Zechariah, for your _ _ _ _ _ _ has been heard.

i r a f d a   e r r y a p

Your _ _ _ _ Elizabeth will _ _ _ _ you a _ _ _, and you will _ _ _ _

f e i w   r e b a   n o s   e m a n

him John. You will have _ _ _ and _ _ _ _ _ _ _ _, and many will rejoice

o y j   n e s l a g d s

at his _ _ _ _ _, for he will be _ _ _ _ _ _ in the sight of the _ _ _ _.

t i r h b   r e t a g   r o d L

He will turn _ _ _ _ of the people of Israel to the _ _ _ _ their God.

a m y n   d r L o

He will go _ _ _ _ _ _ them, to make ready a _ _ _ _ _ _ prepared for

f e b e o r   p l e e p o

the Lord."

See Luke 1:13-14, 16-17, NRSV

Memory Verse
Jesus replied, "What is impossible with man is possible with God."
Luke 18:27

Lesson 17: Jesus Choosing His Disciples

Aim: To remember that God calls each of us to be His disciples on a daily basis. We do not need to have any specific talents or gifts because God will provide us the gifts and talents that we need to serve him.

Opening Prayer: Dear Lord Heavenly Father, we thank you for being a God who loves us even though we are not worthy. Thank you for choosing each of us to be disciples just as you called your 12 disciples. Lord, help us to follow you without hesitation and help us to follow you whenever you need us to go and do. Amen.

Let's Read more about the story from the Bible!
  Matthew 4:18-22

[18] As Jesus was walking beside the Sea of Galilee, he saw two brothers, Simon called Peter and his brother Andrew. They were casting a net into the lake, for they were fishermen. [19] "Come, follow me," Jesus said, "and I will send you out to fish for people." [20] At once they left their nets and followed him.

[21] Going on from there, he saw two other brothers, James son of Zebedee and his brother John. They were in a boat with their father Zebedee, preparing their nets. Jesus called them, [22] and immediately they left the boat and their father and followed him.

49

Main Ideas from the Lesson
  1. Jesus called regular fisherman to follow Him.
  2. Jesus said he would make them fishers of men.
  3. Peter, Andrew, James, and John did not hesitate at all when Jesus called them to be his disciples. They immediately left their nets and followed Him.
  4. Just as the disciples followed Jesus when He called them, we too should be willing to follow Jesus in the same way.

Lesson Review:
1. In the lesson passage, Jesus called _____,

_____, _____ and

_____ as his disciples.

2. All of these men were _____.

3. Jesus told them "Come _____ _____."

4. They immediately left their _____ and followed

_____.

Values for Life
•   God does not call the qualified, he qualifies the called. Hence, He chose fishermen, unqualified, to be his disciples. We do not have to be the best at anything, we just have to decide to follow Him and be His disciple every day.
•   When Jesus calls us, we must follow without hesitation.

Life Response/My Decision
I will follow Jesus in my daily life. I will pray that God use me in my school, in my family and at my church. I will try my best to be a disciple in the ways that I act, the decisions that I make, and the words that I say.

12 Disciple Crossword Puzzle

```
J P L A K O D J P J B G P O A
X B E B Y I R I Z A J Z Q M M
C Z T T S C L M R M A L T C I
H F Y I E I O T Q E M N M S X
Z K M C H R H H L S E I H P J
Y O D P U O H Q T A S D Z O U
N Y R E L V E I H L K W F B J
W D U O H R G V F P C R W W O
R E M D C F Y X J H Y R E L W
G E H S U E A D D A H T R G J
W H R T H O M A S E G V D T A
G Y K D T V S A D U J Q N E R
C O O H B A L A C S O N A G E
I L Z O I D M B J I D H D S C
H O N Q X G Y E I A Q J H D U
```

ANDREW
BARTHOLOMEW
JAMES
JAMES ALPHAEUS
JOHN
JUDAS
MATTHEW
PETER
PHILIP
SIMON
THADDAEUS
THOMAS

Memory Verse

"Come, follow me," Jesus said, "and I will send you out to fish for people."

Matthew 4:19

Lesson 18: Centurion's Servant

Aim: To remember that God is the ultimate Healer and that we can have faith that He hears our prayers when we pray for others and ourselves for healing from sickness, physical, mental, or emotional.

Opening Prayer: Dear Lord Heavenly Father, we pray that you be with us as we learn about the faith of the Centurion. Lord help us to have faith like him when we pray for other's healing. Help us to trust you and believe that you are a God who hears our prayers. Amen.

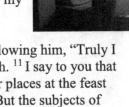

Let's Read more about the story from the Bible!
Matthew 8:5-13

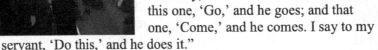

[5] When Jesus had entered Capernaum, a centurion came to him, asking for help. [6] "Lord," he said, "my servant lies at home paralyzed, suffering terribly." [7] Jesus said to him, "Shall I come and heal him?"[8] The centurion replied, "Lord, I do not deserve to have you come under my roof. But just say the word, and my servant will be healed. [9] For I myself am a man under authority, with soldiers under me. I tell this one, 'Go,' and he goes; and that one, 'Come,' and he comes. I say to my servant, 'Do this,' and he does it."

[10] When Jesus heard this, he was amazed and said to those following him, "Truly I tell you, I have not found anyone in Israel with such great faith. [11] I say to you that many will come from the east and the west, and will take their places at the feast with Abraham, Isaac and Jacob in the kingdom of heaven. [12] But the subjects of the kingdom will be thrown outside, into the darkness, where there will be weeping and gnashing of teeth."

[13] Then Jesus said to the centurion, "Go! Let it be done just as you believed it would." And his servant was healed at that moment.

Main Ideas from the Lesson

1.   A centurion came to Jesus with great faith on behalf of his servant who was paralyzed and suffering.
2.   Jesus wanted to come to the man's house, but the centurion said that just Jesus' word can heal the servant man.
3.   The centurion understood the power of Jesus' authority and had faith in Jesus.
4.   Jesus healed the man with just his word because of the centurion's great faith.

Lesson Review:

1. Jesus entered _____ when a _____ came to him for help.

2. The centurion had a servant at home _____ and suffering.

3. Jesus said "Shall I _____ and _____ him?"

4. The centurion just wanted Jesus' _____ for his servant to be healed because he knew of Jesus' great power.

5. The _____ was healed with just Jesus' word.

Explain the similarities between the centurion's role in his job and how he understood that Jesus only had to say to be healed and the servant would be healed.

Values for Life

1. When we pray, we must pray with faith, knowing that God is hearing our prayers.
2. It is important that we pray for others who need help from God, the ultimate Healer. We must take the time to intercede for others and be there for them in their time of need.

Life Response/My Decision

I will take the time to pray for others, especially those who need healing from physical, mental, or emotional sickness. I will pray with faith knowing that our God hears our prayers and is a Healer. With our true faith and obedience, God can do miracles.

Centurion's Servant Crossword

Across
3. "But say the word, and my servant will be _____."
5. The commander loved the nation and built their _____.
7. The commander understood that Jesus had _____ over sickness.
9. A commander of soldiers
10. The town Jesus went to

Down
1. How the servant was when the friends returned
2. The person who was dying
4. Sent to ask Jesus to help
6. Jesus was amazed at the man's great _____.
8. The commander sent friends to tell Jesus not to _____ himself to come to his house.

Memory Verse

"We know that all things work together for good for those who love God, who are called according to his purpose."

Romans 8:28

Lesson 19: Sick man at the pool of Bethesda

Jesus has the power to heal us.

Aim: To remember that God is always listening to our needs and that He has the power to heal us in His perfect timing in our lives.

Opening Prayer: Dear Lord Heavenly Father, we thank you for being a God who love us and still heals us from problems. Help us to reflect on the story of the sick man at the pool and help us to remember how you healed him and will also heal us. Amen.

Let's Read more about the story from the Bible! John 5:1-15

Some time later, Jesus went up to Jerusalem for one of the Jewish festivals. [2] Now there is in Jerusalem near the Sheep Gate a pool, which in Aramaic is called Bethesda and which is surrounded by five covered colonnades. [3] Here a great number of disabled people used to lie—the blind, the lame, the paralyzed[5] One who was there had been an invalid for thirty-eight years. [6] When Jesus saw him lying there and learned that he had been in this condition for a long time, he asked him, "Do you want to get well?"

[7] "Sir," the invalid replied, "I have no one to help me into the pool when the water is stirred. While I am trying to get in, someone else goes down ahead of me." [8] Then Jesus said to him, "Get up! Pick up your mat and walk." [9] At once the man was cured; he picked up his mat and walked. The day on which this took place was a Sabbath, [10] and so the Jewish leaders said to the man who had been healed, "It is the Sabbath; the law forbids you to carry your mat."

[11] But he replied, "The man who made me well said to me, 'Pick up your mat and walk.' " [12] So they asked him, "Who is this fellow who told you to pick it up and walk? [13] The man who was healed had no idea who it was, for Jesus had slipped away into the crowd that was there. [14] Later Jesus found him at the temple and said to him, "See, you are well again. Stop sinning or something worse may happen to you." [15] The man went away and told the Jewish leaders that it was Jesus who had made him well.

Main Ideas from the Lesson

1. In Jerusalem there is a pool called Bethseda at which many disabled persons used to lie.
2. When Jesus saw one of the men Jesus asked him "Do you want to get well?"
3. The man at the pool stated that he wants to but no one wanted to help him into the pool.
4. Jesus said to him "Ge up! Pick up your mat and walk." And the man was cured and walked.
5. The Jewish leaders were wondering who healed this man on Sabbath and later the man at the pool told them it was Jesus.
6. Jesus warned the man to stop sinning or something worse may happen to him.
7. Jesus is God and He has authority over illnesses.

Lesson Review:

1. Jesus was in the city of _____ to observe a feast.

2. There was a pool called _____ by the Sheep Gate.

4. The man in the story had not been able to walk for _____ years.

5. Jesus told the man to pick up his _____ and

_____.

6. The Jews became angry because Jesus had _____ the

man on the _____.

7. The man did not know who had helped him because Jesus walked away into the

_____.

8. When Jesus saw the man again, he told him to stop _____ or something worse would come upon him.

Values for Life

1. There are times in our lives that the only person we can call on or ask for help is Jesus. This is okay because we have Jesus to be our healer, our provider, the one who loves us more than everyone.
2. We must take our requests to God.
3. We must have faith that God can heal us on any day as long as it glorifies God.

4. God can heal our lives whether we have physical, emotional, or mental sickness.

Life Response/My Decision

I will take my problems, my sickness, and my joys in life to Jesus. I will trust that God hears my prayers and that He can heal my life if I trust Him and have faith.

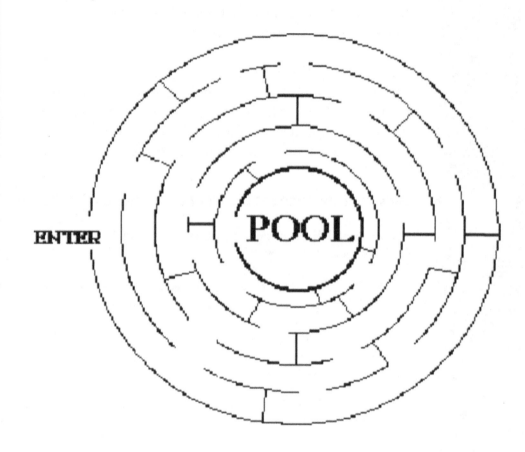

ENTER

POOL

Memory Verse

Then Jesus said to him, "Get up! Pick up your mat and walk." At once the man was cured; he picked up his mat and walked. The day on which this took place was a Sabbath. –John 5;8-9

Lesson 20: Huge Catch of Fish

Jesus calls us to be fishers of men.

Aim: To remember that Jesus called ordinary men to be fishers of men and that ministry is dependent on God.

Opening Prayer: Dear Lord Heavenly Father, we thank you for choosing each of us, ordinary people to be disciples, even when we are not worthy. Help us to believe in you everyday and to follow you through our life, through our words, and through our actions. Help us to obey you when you call us to be fishers of men. Amen.

Let's Read more about the story from the Bible! Luke 5:4-11

[4] When he had finished speaking, he said to Simon, "Put out into deep water, and let down the nets for a catch."

[5] Simon answered, "Master, we've worked hard all night and haven't caught anything. But because you say so, I will let down the nets."

[6] When they had done so, they caught such a large number of fish that their nets began to break. [7] So they signaled their partners in the other boat to come and help them, and they came and filled both boats so full that they began to sink.

[8] When Simon Peter saw this, he fell at Jesus' knees and said, "Go away from me, Lord; I am a sinful man!" [9] For he and all his companions were astonished at the catch of fish they had taken, [10] and so were James and John, the sons of Zebedee, Simon's partners.

Then Jesus said to Simon, "Don't be afraid; from now on you will fish for people." [11] So they pulled their boats up on shore, left everything and followed him.

Main Ideas from the Lesson

1. Jesus went to ordinary people like Simon, and called them to be fishers of men.
2. Jesus told Simon to put out his net again, but Simon was doubtful, but still obeyed what Jesus told him to do.
3. When they saw how many fish they caught they were amazed.
4. Simon felt unworthy to be near Jesus because he was sinful, but Jesus told him not to be scared and that he would fish for men from now on.

Although we don't use a real net to bring people to Jesus he does want us to go out *and "catch" people and* bring them in the Kingdom. There are many things we can do to be good fishers of people. We can show love and care to other people. We can tell them about Jesus and his wonderful love. We can pray for them. And we can invite them here to church where they can experience some of the love and joy of the *family of God. With the Holy Spirit's help they just might decide to be followers of* Jesus, just like the rest of us fish!

Lesson Review:

1. What did Jesus ask Simon to do? .

2. Jesus didn't tell Simon that he would catch any more fish, but Simon still listened to Jesus and let the net down. What happened when Simon let the net down?

3. What did Jesus tell the men at the end of the story?

4. What does it mean to be a fisher of men?

Values for Life
- Jesus calls ordinary people to do extraordinary things for the expansion of His Kingdom.
- Each of us are called to be fishers of men, to tell others about Jesus.
- We must obey Jesus in our daily lives and follow Him and the way that He lived His life.
- We don't have to be afraid when God is in control of our lives.

Life Response/My Decision

I will be a fisher of men by living a life like Jesus did and to reflect his love to others around us. I will not be afraid to follow Him because I know that He is in control of my life.

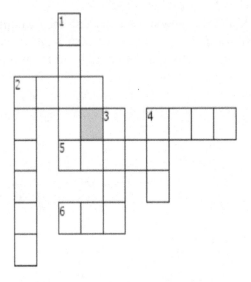

ACROSS

2. An animal which lives in water and is covered with scales
4. To go down below the surface of the water
5. The land along the edge of an ocean, sea, lake, or river
6. An openwork fabric of cords used to catch fish

DOWN

1. The Son of God
2. To get behind someone and go where they go
3. A small vehicle for traveling on water
4. A large area of water, smaller than an ocean

Jesus	net	fish	sink
shore	boat	sea	follow

Memory Verse

Then Jesus said to Simon, 'Don't be afraid; from now on you will catch men. –Luke 5:10

Lesson 21: Temple Cleansing

Aim: I will be able to explain why GOD's house is HOLY and a place to be treated with respect.

Opening Prayer: FATHER, help us to remember that we are Your temple and that Your Spirit lives in us. Help us to keep our lives clean and useful for service to You. In Jesus' name we pray. AMEN.

Let's Read more about the story from the Bible!
Mark 11: 15-18

Jesus Cleanses the Temple

[15] Then they came to Jerusalem. And he entered the temple and began to drive out those who were selling and those who were buying in the temple, and he overturned the tables of the money changers and the seats of those who sold doves; [16] and he would not allow anyone to carry anything through the temple. [17] He was teaching and saying, "Is it not written,

'My house shall be called a house of prayer for all the nations'?

But you have made it a den of robbers."

[18] And when the chief priests and the scribes heard it, they kept looking for a way to kill him; for they were afraid of him, because the whole crowd was spellbound by his teaching.

Things to Remember: Main ideas from the lesson

We celebrate many important events in our lives. Think of all the celebrations that you've been a part of in your life, birthdays, weddings, Holidays, and New Year to name a few. Each big event has special ceremonies attached to them. For birthdays, we blow out candles on cakes; for New Year we see fireworks. In Jesus' time, Passover was a time of celebration! The people of Jerusalem made a really big deal about it. It was traditional for a Jewish man to travel to Jerusalem to worship God and participate in Passover ceremonies.

Jesus was a big fan of Passover. He respected all the traditions that went along with Passover and respected the Temple it was celebrated at. The Temple, like our Church, was a holy place and everyone who went there treated it with respect. Back in Jesus' time, the temple used to have a special room that had the "Ark of the Covenant" in it. The "Ark of the Covenant" is a gold covered wooden chest that contained the tablets of stone with the ten commandments inscribed on it. Moses built it as a symbol of GOD's presence with his people, the Israelites. This is what made the temple even more holy and special!

Think about some things we are not allowed to do inside our Church sanctuary? Why do you think that is?

Swiffer mops, vacuum cleaners...what are these things used for? I hope you said to clean house! What clues do we get when we need to clean our house? Well, today we're going to learn about a time that Jesus did some house cleaning...err...I mean temple cleaning!

Jesus had been celebrating Passover his whole life and traveling with his family to Jerusalem. This time, his disciples had joined him on his journey to Jerusalem. As Jesus got closer to the Temple, he noticed that things were different. Which might be normal if you had not visited a place in a long time. Jesus was a man used to change, but what he saw made him very upset!

He did NOT see people worshipping God as was the tradition. Instead, the temple looked like a big market! It was loud with animal sounds and people talking and selling things for money. They were taking advantage of the Passover celebration by charging people from out of town a lot of money for things. Think about all the times you went on vacation with your family and spent so much money on Souvenirs that you could probably buy at the Dollar store for cheaper.

Jesus was very sad and angry. He could not believe how people were treating God and God's place of worship. He couldn't just stand around and do NOTHING!

People must have thought Jesus was crazy when he chased the merchants out of the temple and scared the animals away. He flipped over the tables where things were being sold. Everyone was shocked at the way Jesus reacted, but Jesus cleaned house at the temple that day!

Jesus wanted to put things back the way it was supposed to be. To turn the Temple back to a place of worship that is respected by everyone.

Lets Review!

1. What were the Jewish People doing at the temple?

_____

_____

_____

2. What made Jesus angry?

_____

_____

_____

3. What does it mean to "cleanse" the temple?

_____

_____

_____

Values for Life

As we think about Jesus cleansing the temple, we should remember that the Bible tells us that we are the "temple of GOD" and that GOD's spirit lives in us. The season of LENT is a good time for us to really think about what we want to cleanse in ourselves.

Life Response/My Decision

I will pick one thing that I want to "cleanse" in myself and work on that during LENT season. I will also work to keep my church clean and respect it as Jesus would expect me to.

> **Memory Verse**
>
> 'Don't you know that you yourselves are GOD's temple? GOD's spirit lives in you.
>
> 1 Corinthians 3:16

Lesson 21: Temple Cleansing

Activity 1: TEMPLE TELEPHONE

Have the children stand in a straight line.

Give the first child in the line a piece of paper with an item from today's lesson that needed to be cleaned. (selling doves, sheep, cattle; exchanging money).

By using a paper towel tube, the first child will whisper what is written on the slip of paper through the tube to the next child. Each child will then whisper into the telephone (tube) to the next player until the last child has heard what was whispered through the temple tube.

That child will say the words out loud and see if it is the same word that was written on the slip of paper.

Play again with another player beginning the TEMPLE TELEPHONE.

Encourage children to use words that they can think of for areas in our own lives that need to be cleaned (such as our speech, our prayer life, our obedience, what our eyes watch, or what our ears listen to, etc.

Activity 2: Word Jumble

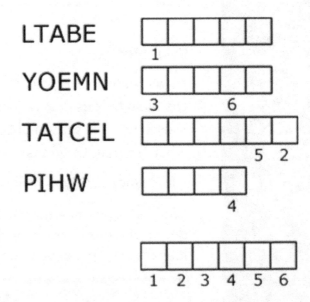

LTABE

YOEMN

TATCEL

PIHW

Lesson 22: Zacchaeus

Aim: I will be able to outline how Jesus accepted, included and loved everyone and list the ways that I can do the same.

Opening Prayer: FATHER, thank you for loving me with all your heart. Teach me to accept, forgive, and love others in the way that you do for me. AMEN.

Let's Read more about the story from the Bible!
Luke 19:1-10 (NRSV)

Jesus and Zacchaeus

19 He entered Jericho and was passing through it.[2] A man was there named Zacchaeus; he was a chief tax collector and was rich. [3] He was trying to see who Jesus was, but on account of the crowd he could not, because he was short in stature. [4] So he ran ahead and climbed a sycamore tree to see him, because he was going to pass that way. [5] When Jesus came to the place, he looked up and said to him, "Zacchaeus, hurry and come down; for I must stay at your house today." [6] So he hurried down and was happy to welcome him. [7] All who saw it began to grumble and said, "He has gone to be the guest of one who is a sinner." [8] Zacchaeus stood there and said to the Lord, "Look, half of my possessions, Lord, I will give to the poor; and if I have defrauded anyone of anything, I will pay back four times as much." [9] Then Jesus said to him, "Today salvation has come to this house, because he too is a son of Abraham. [10] For the Son of Man came to seek out and to save the lost."

Things to Remember: Main ideas from the lesson

Ever been to a show or event where you were not in the front and couldn't see anything because so many people in front of you were taller than you and blocking the view? What could solve this problem? What are some things that you would do so you could see what was going on?

Today's lesson is about a man named Zacchaeus who found out that someone famous was coming to town. Obviously, Jesus is the celebrity in this story. You see, Jesus was famous because he was performing miracles all over town. He raised a man (Lazarus) from the dead and restored the sight of a blind man to name a few of his famous miracles. People were going crazy over Jesus! Crowds gathered everywhere that he went. Everyone wanted to either see Jesus perform something awesome or needed him to help them.

Who was Zacchaeus? Well, he's not the celebrity of this story but he sure is the main character. You see, Zacchaeus was a Jewish man who worked as the "chief tax collector" for the Romans. It's safe to say that many people did NOT like him because he collected their hard earned money from them and even took a more than he was supposed to. This made Zacchaeus a very rich man, but Zacchaeus was NOT a tall man. He really wanted to see Jesus but no one would let him through to see him, so Zacchaeus climbed the nearest and tallest tree, a Sycamore tree, to see Jesus above the crowd.

Have you ever climbed something? What's it like?

As Jesus was passing by below the Sycamore tree, he looked up and saw Zacchaeus looking down at him. He called out to him and said, "Zacchaeus, hurry and come down; for I must stay at your house today."

The people in the crowd were in shock! Jesus wants to go to the house of THIS man who basically robs every one of their hard earned money?! This did not make Jesus popular. People were angry and disappointed that a man this famous wanted to go visit a thief.

Read verse 9 and 10 to find out exactly WHY Jesus chose to go to Zacchaeus' house.

No one knows what Jesus and Zacchaeus talked about but Jesus was able to change his heart. Zacchaeus was so humbled that Jesus made time to talk to him of all people that he decided to change his ways. Jesus forgave Zacchaeus of his sins and this inspired Zacchaeus to do give back half of everything he had to the poor and give back 4 times as much as he stole.

Zacchaeus' curiosity and willingness to come to Jesus changed his life forever. Jesus knew all about Zacchaeus, just like he knows everything about us

Lesson 22: ZACCHAEUS

Let's Review!

1. Why did Zacchaeus climb a tree?

_____

_____

_____

2. How did Jesus make Zacchaeus feel included and/or accepted?

_____

_____

_____

3. How did Zacchaeus repent for his sins?

_____

_____

_____

Values for Life

Even though other Zacchaeus was not a nice man and people did not like him, Jesus still loved him and wanted him to feel included and accepted. Jesus wants us to treat everyone with love and respect, even people we don't like.

Life Response/My Decision

I will be kind to everyone and treat everyone with love and respect even if they are not kind to me.

> ### Memory Verse
> "For the Son of Man came to seek out and save the lost."
> --- Luke 19: 10

Lesson 22: ZACCHAEUS

Activity 1: SIN VS. FORGIVENESS

Materials: Chart paper and Markers

Write the word SIN in big letters with "BIG PROBLEM" (in red) written underneath and on the other chart paper write FORGIVENESS with "BIG ANSWER" (in red) written underneath.

Have the children write the different ways that we sin under the SIN column and the different ways that we forgive under the FORGIVENSES column and discuss how this relates to the story of Zacchaeus

Activity 2: Word Jumble

Zacchaeus

Jericho
Publicans
Rich
Jesus
Little
Sycomore
House
Joy
Poor
Abraham
Salvation
Sinner

Make all the words fit into this crossword

Lesson 23: I AM...

Aim: I will be able to talk about Jesus through His stories in order to get to know Him better.

Opening Prayer: FATHER, thank you for loving me with all your heart. Teach me to accept, forgive, and love others in the way that you do for me. AMEN.

Let's Read more about the story from the Bible!
Matthew 16: 13-20 (NRSV)

Peter's Declaration about Jesus

¹³ Now when Jesus came into the district of Caesarea Philippi, he asked his disciples, "Who do people say that the Son of Man is?" ¹⁴ And they said, "Some say John the Baptist, but others Elijah, and still others Jeremiah or one of the prophets." ¹⁵ He said to them, "But who do you say that I am?" ¹⁶ Simon Peter answered, "You are the Messiah, the Son of the living God." ¹⁷ And Jesus answered him, "Blessed are you, Simon son of Jonah! For flesh and blood has not revealed this to you, but my Father in heaven. ¹⁸ And I tell you, you are Peter, and on this rock I will build my church, and the gates of Hades will not prevail against it. ¹⁹ I will give you the keys of the kingdom of heaven, and whatever you bind on earth will be bound in heaven, and whatever you loose on earth will be loosed in heaven." ²⁰ Then he sternly ordered the disciples not to tell anyone that he was the Messiah.

Things to Remember: Main ideas from the lesson

Who am I? What are all the names that someone might call me?

Everyone knows everyone else by their name or they can describe them by the way they look, what they wear or who they know.

Who is Jesus? How do you know?

69

Open your bibles to Matthew 16. We're going to read verses 13-20 to answer the Lesson Review Questions!

I'm going to name a few names and I want you to describe them to me. If anyone finds a mistake or wants to help, then chime in.

Walt Disney, Barak Obama, Selena Gomez, Ronald McDonald, George Washington, your parish Priest/Achen, LeBron James, Serena Williams

The people we just described are either famous or important but they're not very easy to describe. In today's lesson, people were talking about Jesus as if He was someone great, like John the Baptist or one of the prophets. What they didn't know or understand was that Jesus was even more important and greater than they thought! Jesus was the Messiah, the Son of God!

Someone who we think someone is and who they really are, are very different. Even what we read in the news and on Google tells us very little.

This is NOT the case with Jesus. Jesus was teaching his disciples about himself for THREE years, slowly letting people know that He was their Savior. When Peter said, "You are the Messiah, the Son of the living God." Jesus pretty much said 'You're right!' Peter was the only one who paid attention and realized who Jesus was.

From Jesus' stories in the Bible, we can learn who He really is, which will help us talk about God more easily.

What are some names that you have heard people use to talk about Jesus?

Let's Review!

1. What is the first question that Jesus asked?

_____

_____

_____

2. What is the second question that Jesus asked?

_____

_____

_____

_____

3. Are the two questions different or the same?

_____

_____

_____

4. What did Peter say?

_____

_____

_____

5. What was Jesus' response to Peter?

_____

_____

_____

Values for Life

We are all children of GOD! Each and every one of us is loved by Him, which is the most important part of who we are. Talking about GOD and spreading his word is how we'll really get to be closer to knowing GOD.

Life Response/My Decision

I will practice talking about God to better know him and about him.

> ### Memory Verse
>
> "You are the Messiah, the Son of the living God."
>
> --- Matthew 16:16

Peter's Confession of Christ

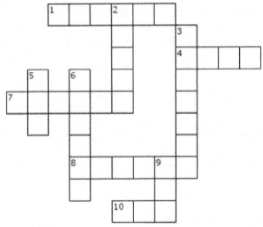

ACROSS

1. Persons; men, women, and children; human beings
4. A large stone that sticks up out of the ground or the sea
7. A male parent
8. The Messiah, as foretold by the prophets
10. An adult male human being

DOWN

2. The name that Jesus called Simon
3. A persons who speaks for God
5. To speak
6. The whole body of believers in Christ
9. A male child in relation to his parents

PETER	FATHER	PEOPLE	SON	CHRIST
PROPHET	ROCK	MAN	CHURCH	SAY

Lesson 23: I AM...

Lesson 24: Team Goat vs. Team Sheep

Aim: To understand that Life is not always fair or equal for everyone. Those who demonstrate **unwavering faith** in HIM will be rewarded.

Opening Prayer: LORD, there is so much we do not understand in this world. Why some people suffer while others seem to have an easier life. It is not for us to question why, but rather know that YOU have a greater purpose for us. Teach me to love YOU by loving others. AMEN.

Let's Read more about the story from the Bible!
Matthew 25: 31-46 (NRSV)

The Judgment of the Nations

[31] "When the Son of Man comes in his glory, and all the angels with him, then he will sit on the throne of his glory. [32] All the nations will be gathered before him, and he will separate people one from another as a shepherd separates the sheep from the goats, [33] and he will put the sheep at his right hand and the goats at the left. [34] Then the king will say to those at his right hand, 'Come, you that are blessed by my Father, inherit the kingdom prepared for you from the foundation of the world; [35] for I was hungry and you gave me food, I was thirsty and you gave me something to drink, I was a stranger and you welcomed me, [36] I was naked and you gave me clothing, I was sick and you took care of me, I was in prison and you visited me.' [37] Then the righteous will answer him, 'Lord, when was it that we saw you hungry and gave you food, or thirsty and gave you something to drink? [38] And when was it that we saw you a stranger and welcomed you, or naked and gave you clothing? [39] And when was it that we saw you sick or in prison and visited you?' [40] And the king will answer them, 'Truly I tell you, just as you did it to one of the least of these who are members of my family,[a] you did it to me.' [41] Then he will say to those at his left hand, 'You that are accursed, depart from me into the eternal fire prepared for the devil and his angels; [42] for I was hungry and you gave me no food, I was thirsty and you gave me nothing to drink, [43] I was a stranger and you did not welcome me, naked and you did not give me clothing, sick and in prison and you did not visit me.' [44] Then they also will answer, 'Lord, when was it that we saw you hungry or thirsty or

a stranger or naked or sick or in prison, and did not take care of you?' ⁴⁵ Then he will answer them, 'Truly I tell you, just as you did not do it to one of the least of these, you did not do it to me.' ⁴⁶ And these will go away into eternal punishment, but the righteous into eternal life."

Footnotes:
Matthew 25:40 (Greek) *these my brothers*

Things to Remember: Main ideas from the lesson

You've been in this situation before. Ever have your teacher put you in groups? What are some ways that your teacher has grouped you? Did he/she have you count off? Think about how it makes you feel when you get put in groups?

Jesus was talking to a large group of people one day about how to get into Heaven. He told them that they would all be separated into two groups. One group would go to Heaven and the other wouldn't.

Read below: Matthew 25: 34-36.

³⁴ Then the king will say to those at his right hand, 'Come, you that are blessed by my Father, inherit the kingdom prepared for you from the foundation of the world; *³⁵for I was hungry and you gave me food, I was thirsty and you gave me something to drink, I was a stranger and you welcomed me,* *³⁶I was naked and you gave me clothing, I was sick and you took care of me, I was in prison and you visited me.*

The people in this group were super excited! I mean, who wouldn't be? These people get to go to Heaven!! Except, they didn't remember doing all the things that Jesus was talking about. Meeting GOD would be like meeting Justin Bieber or Taylor Swift. And you would definitely remember if GOD asked you for food.

GOD doesn't really need us to feed HIM, give HIM clothes, or make HIM soup, but there are people who do. When we help others who are in need, it's like we're helping GOD. He loves it when we love each other.

Now, remember, there was a second group. Team Goat!

This team was UPSET! **Read what GOD told them in Matthew 25: 41-43**

⁴¹ Then he will say to those at his left hand, 'You that are accursed, depart from me into the eternal fire prepared for the devil and his angels; *⁴²for I* was hungry and you gave me no food, I was thirsty and you gave me nothing to drink, *43* I was a stranger and you did not welcome me, naked and you did not give me clothing, sick and in prison and you did not visit me.'*

Whoa whoa whoa! No one would insult GOD like that! They didn't even get a chance to make food for GOD or buy him clothes. So what was GOD talking about?

Let's break it down! GOD doesn't need us to do anything for HIM, but there are many people out there who do need our help. Everyone needs help sometimes and each one of us is able to provide it. We should be generous in giving others our help with open hearts, having faith that GOD will pick us to be in the "RIGHT" group as a result. When we love our neighbors (or those in need) like ourselves, by helping them with food, clothing, etc., it is just like we're doing it for GOD.

To get on the "RIGHT" team, you have to remain **unwavering in your faith** and show **compassion** to those around you in need. Have faith that even if you feel like no one notices or appreciates your kindness, GOD does.

Lets Review!
1. Who is the King in this Bible passage?

_____

_____

2. What side of the King will the sheep be on? _____

3. Who are the "goats"?

_____

_____

4. Write two to three sentences about what you think, "unwavering faith" means.

_____

_____

_____

_____

Values for Life

If we are to be saved, we must be more like the "sheep" rather than the "goats". It takes more effort and thought to give and be kind to someone than it does to take what is offered or to ignore someone or a situation. Have faith that good deeds are noticed even if they are not recognized.

Life Response/My Decision

I will be kind and help those around me who are in need with all my heart because I know that this pleases GOD. I will have Faith that by doing this without being asked to, will help me get to Heaven.

Memory Verse

'Truly I tell you, just as you did it to one of the least of these who are members of my family, you did it to me.'

--- Matthew 25:40

Activity 1: Love Letters

Create cards of encouragement and send them to one of the following:

St. Jude's Children's Center
Veteran's/Active Military Group
Sister Sunday School
Missions Group(s)
Within your Parish (sick, death in the family, etc.)

COLOR ME

The **Sheep** and the **Goats**

Find your way through the sheep and the goats to the finish.
Matthew 25:31-46

START

FINISH

Lesson 25: Martha & Mary's Place

Aim: To understand the importance of spending time with God despite all the things that distract us in our daily lives.

Opening Prayer: LORD, help me to be more focused and to give the right amount of importance to everything around me. Help me to remember my priorities and put You first in all that I do. AMEN.

Let's Read more about the story from the Bible!
Luke 10:38-42

Jesus Visits Martha and Mary

38 Now as they went on their way, he entered a certain village, where a woman named Martha welcomed him into her home. 39 She had a sister named Mary, who sat at the Lord's feet and listened to what he was saying. 40 But Martha was distracted by her many tasks; so she came to him and asked, "Lord, do you not care that my sister has left me to do all the work by myself? Tell her then to help me." 41 But the Lord answered her, "Martha, Martha, you are worried and distracted by many things; 42 there is need of only one thing. [a] Mary has chosen the better part, which will not be taken away from her."

Footnote:
Luke 10:42 *Other ancient authorities read few things are necessary, or only one*

Things to Remember: Main ideas from the lesson

How many of us put Jesus first? Do we welcome Him like Mary? Or do we give everything else a priority instead?

Think of a single day. There are 24 hours in a day and 7 days in a week. But how many of us can say we spend more than 3 hours with God in the course of the entire week? We watch TV, play video games and even sleep longer than we spend time getting to know God in any given day. That sounds a lot more like Martha's story, doesn't it?

If someone gave up so much for **_our_** lives and died for **_our_** sins, do we not owe Him more than just a few minutes of prayer time at night? Spending time with God in prayer, in song, in studying His word through the Bible will help us to know Him better....and He will know us better too. What could be more important than that?

Lets Review!

1. Who was coming over to Martha's home?

_____

2. What is Martha's sister's name?

_____

3. Why was Martha upset with her sister?

_____

_____

_____

4. What was Jesus' response to Martha?

_____

_____

_____

Values for Life

Dedicate some time away from technology, chores and studies to spend time with God **every day** to build a relationship with HIM.

Life Response/My Decision

Jesus wants to get to know us better. But if we don't spend time with Him and make Him a priority in our life, we will lose sight of what is important. I will spend at least 5 minutes a day spending time with God.

Memory Verse
"Ascribe to the LORD the glory of HIS name; worship the LORD in holy splendor."
--- Psalms 29: 2

Activity 1

Spot the Differences in Mary and Martha
Compare the picture on the left with the picture on right. Circle the 14 things that are different.

Activity 2

(Skit) The Dinner Party

NARRATOR: Martha, Mary and Lazarus are expecting a special guest at their house. They decide to have a dinner party for Jesus who is coming in from out of town. This is how their afternoon goes.

MARTHA: Jesus is coming over dinner. I have so much to do today. I've got to make dinner for a very special guest and cleaning the house will not be easy. Yo Bro, please help me move the furniture around to make more room.

NARRATOR: Lazarus lends Martha a hand moving the table out of the center and over to one side of the room. Then Martha looks for Mary's help.

MARTHA: Mar, I've got the bathrooms. Can you please take care of dusting and organizing the other rooms? Laz, is on vacuum and garbage duty.

80

NARRATOR: All three of them set out to work. But Jesus arrived earlier than expected.

DOORBELL: Ding-dong! Ding-dong! Doink! (doorbell malfunction)

NARRATOR: All three of them rush to the door to open it.

LAZARUS, MARTHA & MARY: Jesus!!!!

LAZARUS: What a pleasant surprise! We weren't expecting you until this evening.

JESUS: My flight landed early. I didn't want to trouble you, so I hopped a cab instead. Uber is great!

MARY: There's no end to modern technology....(giggle).

JESUS: No, there isn't Mary. (smile)

MARTHA: Where's everyone's manners? Come in Jesus. Please have a seat and make yourself comfortable.

LAZARUS: We've invited a few of the guys over for dinner, as well, but they won't get here for another hour or so.

JESUS: That's fine. Gives the four of us more time together.

NARRATOR: Lazarus takes Jesus' bag to the bedroom while Mary directs Jesus to have a seat in the family room. Martha is off to the opposite end of the family room, busy in the kitchen. Mary takes a seat on the floor by Jesus' feet. Lazarus soon joins them. But Martha does not. Instead, she's in the middle of making 4 different appetizers and salad. She hasn't even started on the lasagna.

Jesus tell Lazarus and Mary all about His adventures since He saw them last. Both Lazarus and Mary are astonished and loved listening to Jesus talk. Jesus is a great story teller and often makes people laugh and feel comfortable.

Martha, on the other hand, it getting hotter than the oven. She is fuming that Mary is not helping her in the kitchen so that she too could join them in their laughter. Finally, being done with one of the appetizers, she goes to the family room to offer it to Jesus. She stomps in very angrily.

MARTHA: Jesus, hope You like shrimp.

JESUS: Oh, I do Martha. Thank you! It looks really yummy.

MARY: Yeah, it does.

NARRATOR: Mary reaches for one after Jesus takes His shrimp, but Martha pulls the plate away from her. Lazarus doesn't even try to take one after seeing Martha's reaction. Mary's looks sad.

MARTHA: You don't deserve one after I slaved away in the kitchen by myself.

JESUS: (speaking softly) Martha, don't be angry with Mary for doing what is right. She was looking after me. Isn't that what's important? Looking after your guest's needs? Besides, I came to spend time with all of you. Not necessarily to eat. I've missed you all.

NARRATOR: Jesus draws Martha over to sit on the couch with him.

LAZARUS: Martha, sorry Mary and I didn't consider how much work you were putting into tonight's party. We should have talked it over and helped you sooner.

MARY: The guys will be here soon. Why don't we keep it simple and order pizza and wings instead?

JESUS: Sounds GREAT to me!

NARRATOR: Martha looked relieved and was happy to be able to join them in their conversation and laughter. The disciples and the pizza arrived at the same time. They had a wonderful evening that night...a memory that Martha, Mary and Lazarus would treasure forever.

Made in the USA
Monee, IL
20 September 2024

66281406R00050